S0-AIR-395

# Linguistic Concepts

KENNETH L. PIKE

# Linguistic Concepts

**An Introduction to**

**Tagmemics**

University of Nebraska Press   Lincoln and London

Portions of Part I appeared originally in
*Reading about Language*, by Charlton Laird
and Robert M. Gorrell,
copyright 1971 by Harcourt Brace Jovanovich, Inc.

Copyright 1982 by the
University of Nebraska Press

Manufactured in the United States of America

The paper in this book meets the guidelines for
permanence and durability of the
Committee on Production Guidelines for
Book Longevity of the Council on
Library Resources.

Library of Congress Cataloging in Publication Data

Pike, Kenneth Lee, 1912-
Linguistic concepts.

Bibliography: p.
Includes index.
1. Tagmemics.   I. Title
P160.P48   415   81-19814
ISBN 0-8032-3664-6   AACR2

# Contents

# Figures

# Preface

In this volume *person* (and relation between persons) is given theoretical priority above formalism, above pure mathematics, above idealized abstractions.

A person, as observer, has choice. This choice extends to adoption of a theory or a temporary or permanent combination of theories (see Chapter 1). A theory may be adopted because it is exciting to the observer, is useful to reach some material or cultural goal, or helpful to understand oneself, others, or one's environment.

In the theory surveyed here (see Chapter 2, for summary), discussion begins (Part I) with observer variableness. One can choose to see the world as made up largely of discrete bits, particles (Chapter 3). This has the advantage of obviousness, since well-known "things" serve as the model for extension to less easily observed units, and the relation of one unit joined to another to make a larger thing is also close to experience. The danger is that the analyst will get carried away with its usefulness and assume that the world is *nothing but* discreteness—a partitioning—of nonoverlapping elements. But fusion, merging, gradients, change, growth, education, and indeterminacies are also a part of experience and are difficult to capture if only a particle theory is available.

In order to meet this need, the theory adds the perspective of wave (Chapter 4). The merging of units and the overlapping of borders are to be expected, and not to be treated as a theoretical disturbance. But there is no suggestion here that *some* items are particles, while others are waves; rather, *any* particle can be viewed (for certain temporary purposes) as a wave, and *any* wave can be viewed (for other temporary purposes) as a particle.

Similarly, *all* events or situations or items or components or persons can for certain purposes of the observer be viewed for a time as points in a set of relationships (that is, as making up a field, Chapter 5). The relationships between these points or things or events or persons can be focused on as comprising one view of reality. But here also the emphasis must be repeated that when life and the universe are viewed as *nothing but* relationships, without adequate provision for viewing the world of man as made up of particles and waves, insurmountable difficulties will eventually be encountered. And again, the solution is not to treat *some* elements as relations and *others* as units, but to be able to use all three approaches as alternative ways to view *every* situation as static, dynamic, or relational according to the current needs and interests of the observer.

In Part II, emphasis shifts to the units themselves. Yet even here the hopeless attempt to eliminate the observer in favor of scientific detachment or of objectivity is dismal. Units must be experienced or observed or deduced or imagined. In language, combinations of features are units, to human view, only when there is purpose, meaning, relevance, or significance of some kind to give coherence to a set of sensations or memories or involvements or imaginations. Unless one item is perceived as *different* from another (tacitly, by no means necessarily explicitly), it cannot be treated as a separate unit (Chapter 6); and only when such differences are present are the features involved serviceable as identificational features for units in the absence of such contrasting units.

Similarly, every repeatable or identifiable unit of human experience has a range of variation within it, or in the human's perception or experience or imagination of it (Chapter 7). The stance varies, and the sensations with it, even when the flowing river remains the same or the table is still a table. The persistence of units seen via their identificational-contrastive features, along with variableness in these units, forces us to a theoretical position for *all* of rational behavior (not just linguistics). Such a persistent, perceptual unit is termed an *emic* one (drawn from the linguistic term *phonemic*)—an entity seen as "same" from the perspective of the internal logic of the containing system, as if it were unchanging even when the outside analyst easily perceives that change. (Meanwhile, the term *etic*, from the linguistic term *phonetic*, labels the point of view of the outsider as he tries to penetrate a system alien to him; and it also labels some component of an emic unit, or some variant of it, or some preliminary guess at the presence of internal emic units, as seen either by the alien observer or as seen by the internal observer when somehow he becomes explicitly aware of such variants through teaching or techniques provided by outsiders.)

In addition, a physical component is posited for every emic unit of behavior. This adds a further constraint to all possible views of the universe as seen through this theoretical perspective as a whole. No item of human behavior can be completely abstracted from all physical settings, or from all physical components; no purely abstractional system can serve in it, whether of ideas or of postulated systemic relational elements. Each must have its physical component. That is, the theory is *not* completely *mechanistic*, since it has purpose, meaning, significance, and human relevance tied to it; and it is *not* completely *abstract*, since it has a physical component for every emic unit. (For thought itself, the physical component would be composed of some kind of physical activity in the brain.)

Yet along with identificational-contrastive features and variants with physical components, there is a third requirement for the existence of emic units. They must be *appropriate* to some place in a system; they must be appropriately *distributed* (Chapter 8). Random occurrence does not make a system. And man without pattern is not man.

The distributional component, from a different perspective, results—when items are seen as lined up in a structure—in the presence of a relational field. So we already find that there is no partitioning here between distribution and field; they are related concepts used for slightly different purposes under related but different conditions. So also, variants can be seen in relation to merging or growing—and variation overlaps on the dynamic perspective of wave.

Why, then, do we find value in such a multiple perspective? Why not *just one*, kept neatly partitioned into its parts? Life won't allow such isolationism of fact from fact, man from man, view from view, or man from fact and view.

Reductionism is inadequate. We do not have access to the ultimate minimum units; our successors may find even smaller bits of matter or of energy, just as our contemporaries have gone deeper than did those Greeks who talked earlier about atoms. And there are thresholds where the whole cannot be equated to parts in mere combination; hierarchy is needed, with threshold phenomena (see Part III). Then any discipline can enter wherever it chooses, by an arbitrary—human—choice for pleasure or profit, and build upwards to expanding complexity, and downwards to descending complexity (not downward to ultimate simplicity, since the parts are, once more, viewable only by man in system, in structure, in emic relations to causation as deduced by man in man's system—and this is not simple). Biology may choose to enter via a living cell, going up, for example, to man and down to photosynthesis—or something else. In linguistics, I personally choose to enter *not* at the level of the sentence, nor even by use of a feature of a sound (for example, voicing), but at the level of *social interaction* of person with person. This leads directly to dialogue, personal response, and definition of sentence in relation to dialogue (see Chapter 9). It leads also to pronunciation elements such as the relatively isolatable syllable (see Chapter 10). And it opens the door to the systematic study of encyclopedic *particulars* (Chapter 11)—of particular men, particular events, particular tables, particular ideas as seen by man and related to him. Again, it circles back on particles as particular things, or on a background underlying a (tacit) field.

But is such complexity *logically* justifiable? Is only *logical* simplicity to be acceptable to the academic community? Here I quote the logician Susanne K. Langer: "We are no longer limited to propositions that are simple, obvious, and generally entertained. If we chance upon a fairly complex and even surprising proposition, from which very many simple ones would follow, we are perfectly justified in taking the former as a postulate, and deriving the others from it" (1953:185). And: "One's aim in formulating an algebra is always to reach as soon as possible the greatest number of important propositions. Which propositions are 'important' depends upon the *use* one makes of the algebra" (308).

Tagmemic theory—the name for my theory of *unit-in-context* as presented here—is more complex than some theories in demanding that context be considered at every step (Part IV): that is, in all perception and experience and knowledge. Form must not be treated apart from meaning (Chapter 12). Humans perceive forms in relation to situational function, whether that function is perceived in relation to nonhuman cause (a thunderstorm, perhaps), or human cause (a war). In each case, meaning of some kind is present—or else the emic form cannot be perceived. (An unknown object may be perceived emically *as* an *unknown* "thing"—with borders perceived in relation to prior experience.) Similarly, change (Chapter 13) occurs only in relation to some merging of unit with unit, or in relation to a containing field. So, once more, the perspectives of particle and of wave merge with field, with context, with form-meaning composites—and with a universe of discourse (Chapter 14). The last of those approaches field structures from the viewpoint of background system, rather than (usually) concentrating on the relationship of those units explicitly under analytical attention.

Again, an objecting query can be raised: Why so many different ways of approaching related things? And, again, we draw on Langer for our reply—where she tells us that unless we have alternative ways of specifying data relations, we do not have a useful algebra: "The possibility of making deductions from given facts depends so often on the *form* in which these facts are given, that a large supply of interchangeable forms is the first requirement for an interesting system. The establishment of more such forms is, therefore, our first ambition in developing the algebra, and the theorems we are most anxious to prove are such as yield more laws of manipulation" (1953:212).

The approach here is designed to serve in a very wide range of circumstances. The principles have been applied, for example, to football games (Pike 1967a: chap. 4), party games (1967a: sec. 1.2), church services (1967a: chap. 3), a breakfast scene (1967a: sec. 5.2), and—briefly—to society (1967a: chap. 17) as well as to language. Human emic experience is the target, not merely linguistics.

Tagmemic theory developed by accident. I did not set out to develop such a theory. I was involved in training linguistic research workers for the study of preliterate languages. As teachers, we did not know to what part of the world our students might eventually go or to what kind of language. We had to teach them by *general* principles, in part, to be ready for anything. As we became more and more general—and were able to teach more and more in the limited time span, since one principle could be adapted to many different situations by minor adjustment—I felt like a man climbing a mountain. At first he could see a small way; as he climbed higher, he could see farther; at the top, he could suddenly see in *all* directions—not just farther in one direction. This suggests the manner in which I gradually discovered, to my utter surprise (and delight) that the principles selected for linguistics were *equally* applicable to anthropology—and eventually to other phases of human activity.

From 1935 to 1948 I had been largely involved in studying pronunciation—phonetics, phonemics, intonation of American English, tone languages. In 1948 I asked whether or not there might be a "phoneme of grammar"—and if so, whether the concept would be as helpful as the phoneme to those of us investigating preliterate structures. With this question in mind, I eventually worked out contrast, variation, and distribution for the tagmeme (for a while called "grameme," in the first publications of this view in 1954 [Pike 1967a]). Eventually, the analysis of the unit was elaborated into the tagmeme as unit-in-context, with the four cells, as described below in section 9.4.

In 1959 I wanted to reach a more general audience, and used the metaphor of particle, wave, and field to try to do so. It turned out that this view of perspective was very useful as an approach to the observer and his role, to supplement the approach through units. In 1960, further development of approach through field began when I asked whether or not there might be in grammar an analogue of the phonetic chart, but with the chart treated seriously as a legitimate emic unit of the observer; this led to numerous publications helpful in the study of clauses, of affixes, and eventually of discourse itself.

Following the question about a "phoneme of grammar" in 1948, the theory had developed far enough by 1950 that my wife Evelyn began to make up artificial problems to help teach the approach (much as an arithmetic book might have problems about two plus two, without mentioning particular apples). A few of the exercise problems from that year are still preserved in Pike 1967a:212–17.

In 1966, I drafted the present book on concepts, and had half of it mimeographed for classroom use by 1968. But I ran into a major problem: Meaning, although treated in 1967a: 598–640, was not as clearly handled as I needed, if I were to feel comfortable in finishing the book; so I put it to one side for over a decade. In 1971, however, Evelyn and I began a pedagogical text to implement the teaching of the semantic and discourse characteristics of the theory (with exercises to include the kind of work we had done before, but to go beyond it). Here Evelyn had a semantic breakthrough, with "purpose" being added explicitly to the treatment of the events of the referential hierarchy (replacing our older lexical hierarchy, but retaining lexical items as the substance manifesting the new hierarchy). In addition, she pushed the notation for the four-celled tagmeme consistently from the highest levels of discourse down to the morpheme— which I had not myself done. These matters were then included in Pike and Pike 1977, and tested in the classroom for several years both at the University of Michigan and the University of Oklahoma.

With this behind us, I then returned to the present book, seeking once more to try to write for an audience which might be interested in the general principles involved. I wish them enjoyment as they try to read it. They may have to struggle with some of the data and claims, of course, since the views presented may seem to them to be buried in some irrelevant way. But this may often be the price of pleasure. Suppose, for example, that one wants to know the analysis of

WOWOLFOL

It may take a bit of study to see that it hides a wolf in sheep's clothing.

# I

## The Observer and Things

# Introduction to Part I

When man studies "things," he injects part of himself into their definition. What is a chair, if there is no man to sit on it? A flute, with no player? A concert, with no listeners? A saw, with no carpenter? The relevance or intended use of a thing is part of its nature as experienced by us—a component added to it by its designer or user or deduced by an observer.

One approach to studying language emphasizes that man as a user of language affects the nature of the units of his language. His reactions to language become part of the data for the study of language, because described expectations of his reactions are part of the definitions of the structure of language.

The list and kind of things men find will vary radically if they adopt different *theories as tools* with which to search for these units. The theory is part of the observer; a different theory makes a different observer; a different observer sees different things, or sees the same things as structured differently; and the structure of the observer must, in some sense or to some degree, be part of the data of an adequate theory of language. A particular language, of a particular culture, in relation to a particular person with his particular history constitutes an implicit theory for that person.

Tagmemic theory is, in this respect, a theory of theories which tells how the observer universally affects the data and becomes part of the data. No wonder, therefore, that tagmemic theory cannot stop with confining its interest to mere language, but must view language in the broader context of the study of ordinary lay nonverbal behavior as well as in the context of the behavior of that special language observer, the linguist.

Chapter 1 discusses my view of the nature of theory itself. Chapter 2 gives some basic concepts accepted by tagmemic theory as a foundation for its development. Then Chapter 3 discusses the first of three kinds of perspective which the observer can tacitly or explicitly adopt: the view of the universe as made up of *particles*. Chapter 4 covers comparable ground, showing that the *same things* or situations can be viewed *as if* they were *waves*. Chapter 5 changes the perspective to one of field—that is, the same data once more, but this time with units viewed as points or relations in a pattern as part of an even larger system.

# 1

# Theory

"Why study theory? Why not just be practical?" So speak those who fail to realize that the line between theory and practice is blurred—that in many situations only an approach to theory will allow practical results to be obtained in reaching one's goals. Today's practicality is often no more than the accepted form of yesterday's theory.

## 1.1. Value of a Theory

A theory is like a window.

The intellect, in order to get outside itself and to interpret the sense data impinging on the body, needs in advance some kind of idea of the way in which the data may turn out to be organized. Then it can search for pattern.

A theory in this sense is *directional* (see fig. 1.1). By looking out of a south window we get one view, but out of a north window a different view. Both lead to partial insight into one's surroundings, but in different directions. Sometimes, however, the same view may be seen through two different windows. Similarly, different theories may each contribute insight into the nature of patterns of language. If we look at the same data through different theories, we may see different aspects of a pattern.

A theory must be *simpler* than reality if it is to be helpful. It attempts to strip away from attention those items which are not important to the observer *at the moment*. In this way it helps obtain answers to particular

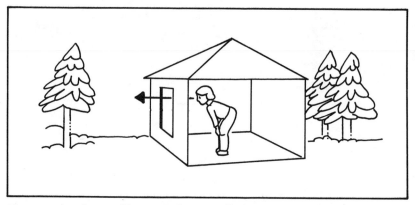

*Figure 1.1. A theory, like a window, can look at only part of the data, and in one direction at a time.*

questions on a narrow front by simplifying the task of investigation. Only if a theory is simpler than that reality which it is in part reflecting is it useful.

In physical situations, a model may be physical—a construction, to scale, which can be destroyed or distorted. The model is less expensive to destroy than the real thing would be. Conceptually, on the other hand, a mathematical model may allow one to manipulate in more detail and more extensively some of the characteristics of reality without interference by other characteristics not built into the model. The relation of two plus three does not need apples—or bridges—to clutter the addition process.

It follows, therefore, that a model allows more *exhaustive* and *systematic* tests for relationships between certain variables than can be handled or isolated with ease in reality itself. By exhausting possibilities of *certain* relationships one can test certain implications of those relationships without the expense involved in trying to test them when other factors interfere.

## 1.2. Weaknesses of a Theory

Any theory may have a weakness at the point of its greatest strength. Since a theory looks in a particular direction, as in the window illustration, it may tell us nothing about data or characteristics of reality which must be seen from some other vantage point. A scientific theory is good only if it *leaves out wisely* those materials which are relevant to other questions but not to those immediately being answered. But the necessary valuable simplicity of a particular theory can destroy its usefulness if it happens to leave out data which are in fact at that moment important. Unfortunately, the observer cannot always be sure what is important; a mistake here will hurt him.

All theories eventually are doomed to be outmoded. A useful theory investigates a point of interest to a particular observer at a particular time. If the theory is successful, that particular problem will have been solved by it. Interest then switches to other problems, requiring further theory. But these other problems are of the deepest kind only if they involve data deliberately or unintentionally left out by the otherwise successful theory. The next stage of investigation requires a model which is more inclusive. When that one, in turn, has made its contribution, it needs to be replaced by another with wider, or different, perspectives which cover other parts of the physical or conceptual universe.

A good theory is like a smooth, clean window. A bad theory may allow us to see, but with excessive distortion, blurring, or a filtering out of some useful information relevant to the task at hand. A window which has wavy glass may distort reality. Nevertheless, if one wishes to look out of a room, one had better have a glass window which is wavy than have no window at all. A dirty window allows one to see something, even though what one sees may be blurred. To have a poor theory is better than having no theory at all.

## 1.3. Selection of a Theory

In trying to choose or to build a theory we should seek an organized, systematic arrangement of general principles which will help us to *understand* something about our physical or conceptual world. We wish for insight into the nature of the setting of our lives, our behavior, and the things with which we must cope.

Since we want a theory to help us, a theory may be viewed as a conceptual tool. A good theory is a *useful* one. Usefulness, in turn, is relevant to some purpose, to some goal. This implies that theories may be good or bad, relative to the sociological setting in which they are found (see fig. 1.2). A dentist's drill and a steam shovel both are useful for excavation, but not at the same spot. Einstein's theory of relativity may not comprise the most profitable mathematics for designing a culvert—but most of the world's traffic at some time rolls over culverts, whether on rails or at an airstrip.

The freight which a linguistic theory may be called on to carry may include the refinement of techniques for teaching foreign languages, the

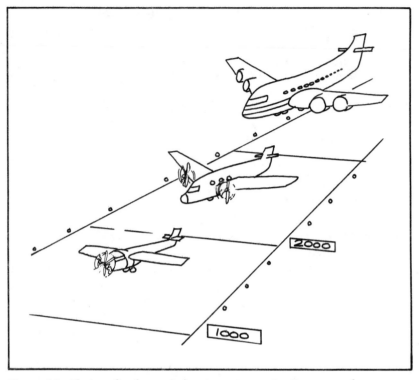

*Figure 1.2. Choice of a theory is in part pragmatic. One may select a theory as one selects an airplane. How far must the plane go? With what load? With what available runways? How expensive is it to obtain? To use? (For this analogy, see Frank 1957:357.)*

preparation of an alphabet for a preliterate culture, the teaching of freshman composition, and the provision of frames of reference to help us understand the relation of language to culture, of language to psychology or philosophy, or of language to life and action.

A theory is most likely to be useful if its results, or predictions, can be easily *tested*. In general, this can be done by two radically different methods: the inductive one works *from* the data toward the theory, and the deductive one works from the theory *toward* the data. Both are useful and effective. In the inductive approach, some available data may be carefully classified as elements appropriate to parts of a guessed-at larger pattern. To test the accuracy of the guess, more data are taken; the analyst then tries to fit these into the pigeonholes of the pattern. If all goes well, one knows he is right—until he is proved wrong.

In a deductive, formal approach, one guesses, to reach an idea of a larger pattern, without worrying much how that pattern was arrived at. Then, to test the hunch, a formal theory is built and used. Such a theory can be thought of as a kind of intellectual machine with three parts: an initial set of axiomatic sentences containing primitive terms, not defined by the theory; secondly, an interpretation, preferably through mathematical formulas which look from these initial statements toward the observed data; and, third, specific predictions about data to be found (compare Carnap 1955:207, 210.) This time one knows one is right—until proved wrong—if a satisfactory number of the data not in hand at the start, but now checked, are just those which the machine predicted should have been there.

A part of the world which we wish to investigate may be likened to a mysterious old castle. One boy may enter it by scaling the high walls; another, by smashing through a sagging door; a third, by crawling through an old escape tunnel. Their first-stage excited reports to each other seem to describe different, unconnected buildings. Later, after they have met somewhere inside the castle, it becomes clear that each *can* find all the areas reported by the others. Each avenue of entrance, however, has its own peculiar directness. To the dungeon? Use the tunnel!

While working with data, all scholars from time to time utilize parts of various underlying theories, not just one. They differ in the proportion of energy devoted to each. In publication, on the other hand, a scholar often, but not always, presents all of his conclusions from just one viewpoint. Logical consistency may appear to him to be desirable in the presentation of results, even if it is impossible during the stages in which the data are being *found* and analyzed.

# 2

## Survey of Tagmemic Theory

### 2.1. Beliefs Underlying Statements

No statement can be made seriously unless preceding it there is in the speaker's thoughts an underlying set of beliefs which he holds firmly, but cannot prove. Ordinary statements and theoretical statements share this restriction. In some sense, man cannot begin with known facts; he has to begin with some kind of commitment, such as the commitment to believe in the existence of facts or the possibility of obtaining knowledge at all.

Often some of the beliefs underlying scientific statements are so far removed from the immediate problem at hand that the speaker does not try to trace them back that far. For example, the scientist normally begins with the belief—which he does not question, and which would not be shaken by an opposing view—that there *is* a world to be investigated. Such beliefs may appear to be common sense. Nevertheless, when a new basic theory is being presented, many of one's older beliefs may be challenged. Occasionally some belief long held will be modified in the face of new kinds of evidence—with far-reaching results in action based upon these beliefs.

When differing scientific views clash, one needs to try to discover what kind of scientific reality, or truth, their authors believe in and start with. This responsibility rests upon us in linguistics; and our particular commitments need to be made explicit for the reader so that he can compare them with implicit or explicit commitments of other scholars. We attempt, therefore, to give here a collection of some of the concepts involved in tagmemic theory. No one basic concept of the theory can be explained (for understanding) or exploited (for usefulness) without reference to each of the others. A theory is, in this sense, a single interlocking whole, just as a circle is not a circle if one part is left out.

**Some Conceptual Tools**

Perspectives as complementary observer standpoints
    Elements seen as particles
    Elements seen as waves
    Elements seen as fields

Units as structured
    With contrastive-identificational components (features)
    With variant manifestations
    With distribution appropriate to class, sequence, and system

Hierarchies of units as parts of wholes
    Phonological
    Grammatical
    Referential

Contexts as relevant
    To form-meaning composites
    To change
    To universe of discourse

*Figure 2.1. A set of interlocking tragmemic concepts which can be thought of as a set of tools for analyzing language and for describing human behavior. Various others (for example, norm, role, nucleus, lexicon, emic) are related to these.*

The concepts presented here are useful for understanding human behavior, including the nature of language, and for finding the structure of that behavior. A number of the most crucial concepts are listed in figure 2.1. Discussion of these in later chapters will make up the principal content of this book. Although many of the problems represented by this list may be traced back to the horizons of history, the synthesis of them given here is new (Pike 1967a); it is given the name *tagmemics*, related to the Greek word from which we get the English word *tactics*; it helps to suggest the *relevant structured arrangement* of *behavioral units* relative to an *insider's* (*emic*) *view* of a behavioral system.

## 2.2. Complementarity of Perspective

Two photographs may appear identical to the casual observer. If, however, these have been taken from vantage points just a few inches apart, and seen separately by the eyes through a stereoscopic arrangement, the brain synthesizes these views into a three-dimensional experience. Similarly, there are three views of linguistics which cover approximately the same material and which in some respects are similar, but which are different enough to allow a far richer experience if the linguist uses all three than if he uses only one. The three-dimensional experience of the stereoscopic view is in part added by the observer, and in some sense is not directly in the flat photographs themselves. Similarly, in language no brute facts are available—all of them are filtered through the receiving mechanisms of the observer. His experience of the factness around him is affected by his perspectives.

Within tagmemic theory there is an assertion that at least three perspectives are utilized by Homo sapiens. On the one hand, he often acts as if he

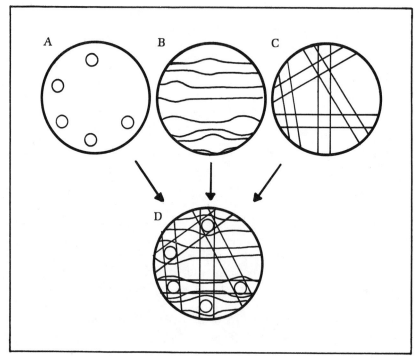

*Figure 2.2. Merging of perspectives in a simple model can show how three different designs can point to the same units. The units can be shown as if they were* isolated *particles (A), or as peaks of* flowing *waves (B), or as points at the intersection of lines (C). All can be superimposed (D), giving the same set of units. The composite enriches our experience of life.*

were cutting up sequences into chunks—into segments or *particles*. At such times he sees life as made up of one "thing" after another. On the other hand, he often senses things as somehow flowing together as ripples on the tide, merging into one another in the form of a hierarchy of little *waves* of experience on still bigger waves. These two perspectives, in turn, are supplemented by a third—the concept of *field* in which intersecting properties of experience cluster into bundles of simultaneous characteristics which together make up the patterns of his experience (see fig. 2.2).

## 2.3. Units as Known

The human being experiences the world around him as made up of *units*. For an element to be treated as a unit it must be considered as *different from* (*in contrast with*) other units. Only those characteristics which make one unit different from another can be used to *identify* that unit. The child knows this, as when he asks, "What is the difference between an elephant and a mailbox?" And adds, "If you don't know, I won't send you to mail my letters!"

In order to know a unit adequately for purposes of identification, we must know the way it *changes* from time to time without ceasing to be itself. How much different can something be and yet not be something else? What are its *variants*? (See fig. 2.3.)

Third, a unit is well known only if one knows where it can appropriately be *found* (its *distribution* must be known). Unless we know where it is *appropriate* for a unit to come, we cannot use it in the right places, and we will appear awkward, unintelligible, or foreign. A noun and a verb, for example, occur at different places in a sentence.

## 2.4. Hierarchy of Interlocking Hierarchies

Man experiences the world as if it were made up of wheels within wheels. Little items are in larger ones, larger ones within still larger ones, until the world becomes one thing after another—larger and larger —or smaller and smaller: "There is a frog on the log in the hole in the bottom of the sea."

In language we find three kinds of hierarchy which are partly independent but which at the same time interlock with each other. In the *grammatical* hierarchy, meaningful lexical chunks make up parts of words entering into larger chunks of structure, which in turn enter into still larger

Susie: 1 year old    Susie: 5 years old    Susie: 13 years old

*Figure 2.3. Units change at different times or places. Talking to Susie appropriately depends upon recognizing both the continuity and change in her personality.*

chunks. At the bottom of this hierarchy are *affixes*—that is, prefixes like *re-* of *return*, or suffixes like *-s* of *returns*, or *roots* like the *turn* of *returns*. These make up words, like *returns*, as a whole; or *phrases* like *will be returning*; or *clauses* like *when the tiger will be returning to his kill*; or *sentences* like *Tomorrow is the time when the tiger will be returning to his kill*; or *paragraphs* discussing a topic announced by such a sentence, developed by further sentences such as *So we better be prepared*. *Monologues* carry long or short speeches of an individual, enclosed in *exchanges* between speaker and hearer, such as:

> *First speaker:*  The tiger will return.
> *Second speaker:* So What?

And *conversations* can carry on further, with various speakers.

On the other hand, the way which a man pronounces may also be arranged in the form of wheels within wheels—smaller items within larger and larger and larger ones. *Cat* is a syllable in which three sounds (spelled *c, a, t*) occur. In the long word *prestidigitator*, however, there may be several syllables, with just one *accented* syllable—which we may call *stressed*—so that the whole word forms a single larger pronunciation unit, that is, one *stress group*. Stress groups become important in the meter of many poems; the *line* sometimes forms a still larger pronunciation unit; and the entire poem, when read aloud, may be pronounced in such a way that a person can tell that the reader is going to stop—evidence that it too is a pronunciation unit of some kind, in the total *phonological hierarchy*.

In addition to the grammatical and phonological hierarchies, we assume (at least in our tagmemic theory, not necessarily in this form in other theories) that there is a *referential hierarchy*. The referential hierarchy includes the *talk-concepts* which people have about *things* and about *events* or about *features* or *situations* relating such things and events, which they *observe*—or *imagine*—and *talk about* (or think about). It is, then, the observed (or imagined) and talked-about reality which is concerning us here. We are simply silent about the "thing-in-itself," which may exist apart from any human observer; things and situations or events enter into our analysis only when *some* perspective is involved. (There is a theistic perspective—of which my own epistemology would be a sample—which would involve an Observer whose hidden-to-us views are not part of our scientific equipment; but such a perspective is relevant to various discussions concerning the nature of reality.)

Identity of a talk-concept referential unit is specified for a particular time and situation by *paraphrase*, that is, by the ability to say the same thing in other ways which the hearer and speaker can agree on as being the same concept for their joint temporary *purposes*. For example, Joey's mother can say to a close neighbor and be understood (but not necessarily successfully by a stranger) *Joey just came home*, or *My boy just arrived*, or *It is my boy who just arrived*, or *My boy just arrived*. Such different ways of saying the same thing include a relevant close similarity of basic content, but often *differ* sharply in terms of *focus* affected by the lexical choice, by grammatical form, or by phonological emphasis. Each of these differences is meaningful, in our view, but attributed to a different hierarchy. And it is important to point out that we do not put into the referential hierarchy the thing or the concept *abstracted* from the speech or the observer. Observer, speech, and experience of thing, situation, or events are kept tied into a package in the units of the referential hierarchy.

## 2.5. Context as Relevant

Language itself can be viewed as action—as a kind of behavior. When people talk to other people, they may wish to influence them to act differently, to believe differently, or to interrelate with them in some social way.

If language did not affect behavior, it could have no meaning. The bits of

*Figure 2.4. The meaning of a word comes from an experience of its behavioral and lexical contexts. The making of a formal dictionary definition comes later, with the lexicographer exploiting some of those contexts.*

forms which we have discussed—sounds, words, sentences—are meaningful not in and of themselves, not just because they exist, but because when used in social environments they do in fact ultimately affect behavior. The meanings grow out of this social relationship. The command *Jump!* implies "jump" only because it has been used in situations where this part of meaning is somehow reacted to vigorously (see fig. 2.4).

   In treating language as behavior, therefore, we first make the point that language elements are *combinations of form and meaning.* We try very hard to avoid studying form by itself or meaning by itself. We deal with them both together. We can never discuss either of them unless, lurking somewhere in the background, is the other. Even when a person tries to talk about the isolated forms of words, he knows that they are meaningful—or he knows that somebody knows that they are meaningful—or he is not handling language. Similarly, if a person tries to make a classification of isolated possible meanings, he is likely to end up without helpful results unless somehow these meanings arise from words which are tied into some language system or systems of cultural behavior (including scientific behavior and its classificatory devices).

Unless one item shares some contextual feature with another, it can have no impact on it—no action on it at an "unconnected" distance. For one man to be able to shoot another, they must belong to the same universe and both be subject to the same physical laws. To talk to one another, men must share some kind of language. *Change involves sharing.*

It is often convenient to speak of a bridge over which change passes—with the bridge being the item or context shared in such a way that it simultaneously belongs to (or contains) the two elements or the two events. Across a river a bridge is shared by both sides (see fig. 2.5). Across a time change, events share the joining moment. The first two sounds of *kitten* smear into one another, by sharing mouth positions part of the time. During the /k/, for example, the middle part of the tongue rises high in the mouth getting ready for the vowel; during the start of the vowel, the back of the tongue is gradually leaving the top of the mouth, where it has closed the mouth for the /k/. The consonant affects the vowel, and the vowel affects the consonant—change works in both directions.

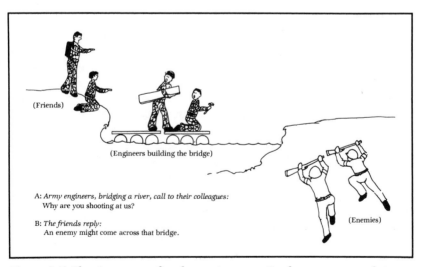

(Friends)

(Engineers building the bridge)

A: *Army engineers, bridging a river, call to their colleagues:*
Why are you shooting at us?

B: *The friends reply:*
An enemy might come across that bridge.

(Enemies)

*Figure 2.5. Sharing occurs for change to occur. So change may work in both directions.*

When one has two words in a row, or several words scattered throughout a paragraph, the mind has to connect them in some way as belonging
to the same area of shared discourse—*a universe of discourse*. Thus *traffic, bridge, automobile, transport,* and the like come under the general
topic of traffic. Similarly, *spring, summer, fall,* and *autumn* are seasons.
*Bicycle, tire, seat,* and *chain* may all be expected to occur in certain kinds
of discussions concerning bicycle repair. These universes of discourse are
determined, not by the words themselves, but by the relationship of the
words to the larger culture within which they are used. A linguistic universe of discourse, therefore, links language and society.

Various linguistic concepts can be illustrated by using this pun: *Did you
know that Robinson Crusoe started the forty-hour week? He got his work
done by Friday.* As a single unit—a joke—it can be viewed as a particle
made up of various smaller particles (including two sentences, for example). It contrasts with other jokes. Referentially, it may be paraphrased in a
variety of ways: *We know that Robinson Crusoe started the forty-hour
week because he got his work done by Friday.* Change from the universe of
discourse of our social structure to that of Crusoe's personal relations occurs over the identity of pronunciation which serves as the bridge which
links the day Friday to the person Friday.

The characteristics of a linguistic theory need to be, insofar as possible,
those which are required by human nature. Tagmemic theory insists that
the efficiency of the brain in using language, and of the child in learning all
kinds of nonverbal patterns of activity, is due to the fact that many of the
deepest principles of the structure of human nature are equally responsible
for activity of nonverbal and verbal types; the child does not have to learn
or utilize a wholly different set of components for his different activities.

A general theory of language is useful in proportion to its exploiting of
these shared features. Tagmemics grew up somewhat like the view which
grows in climbing a large mountain. At first one sees but a short distance in
one direction. As he climbs higher, more of the countryside is in view.
When he reaches the top, he can see in all directions. So also with tagmemic theory. It started with a struggle with a few local linguistic problems. As more languages were tackled and as general principles were
*needed* to analyze languages totally unknown to the linguistic community,
it happened that the practical principles enunciated turned out to cover human behavior in general, that is, it became a theory of language in relation
to a unified theory of the structure of human behavior (see the title of Pike
1967*a*).

# 3

## Particles

### 3.1. Things and Nonthings as "Things"

Human nature experiences the world—sometimes—as made up of *particles*, that is, as "things." Houses, trees, and people seem to be obvious physical objects. But often an experience or concept which obviously is not an object is also talked about *as if* it were one (see fig. 3.1), and is perhaps even counted or measured. Such a concept may be illustrated by the term *movement*, which implies that something is going on; but movements can be counted, like houses (*I saw two houses; I saw two movements*).

An abstraction like *beauty* or *force* can be put in a sentence such as *Beauty is desirable* (as *Food is desirable*); *Some force moved us* or *The bomb moved us*). A *class* of items can be treated as if it were a unit: *the American contingent*. Or a sample of a class can be somehow treated as representing the whole class: *He is the average American*. A symphony may be heard as a unit, even though it may take an hour to play.

Our mental computers seem to be able to operate only if the whole world is processed into bits, each of which can when appropriate be treated as a particle, punched onto our mental IBM cards.

The normal relaxed attitude of the human being in most of his actions treats life as if it were made of particles. Perhaps this is one reason why many people think that a language is just a collection of words one after the other. (Translation, to them, appears merely to require the translator to look up a word in a bilingual dictionary and replace it by the proper equivalent.)

(a melody)

house in decay

(relationship of betweeness)

*cat*

(flowing letters)

(beauty)

thing(s)

process

(force)

*Figure 3.1. Things, processes, and relations can all be viewed as "particles." This provides a static view, in which a melody can be experienced as a unit, even though it takes time; a house, though in the process of falling down, is still a thing; letters of the alphabet are often treated as separate items, even when inseparable in cursive script.*

## 3.2. Particles in Language

In the word *kit* there is a sequence of three units of sound. The first is the pronunciation of /k/. This is the same unit as found at the beginning of *cat* (in spite of the change in spelling) or *character*.

A speech sound is made by the moving parts of the mouth, throat, and lungs. If one takes an X ray moving picture of these motions, a single frame of the movie taken at the central part of the sound gives a static picture of it. In Figure 3.2 /t/ is shown this way.

Words too are particles. They often include within them small particles. The central (*nuclear*) part of a word is the stem, which carries the principal meaning of the word. Smaller parts (affixes) affect the way in which the principal meaning is to be interpreted. In Candoshi of inland Peru (Cox 1957), for example, the word *tayanchshatana* is made up of parts: *ta-ya-nch-sha-t-a-na*. This means 'be-recent-complete-next-individually-I-em-

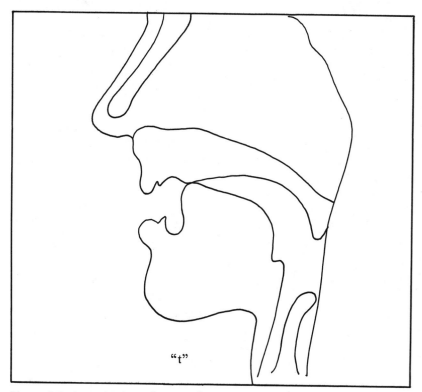

*Figure 3.2. A static view of a sound represents it as one frame from an X-ray moving picture.*

phatically,' or 'I was recently and completely just then individually emphatically there,' or 'I've stayed there then.'

Some language particles are larger than words. If we say *the ugly dog bit the mail carrier,* the whole is a single clause construction, a unit, a particle. The particle *the ugly dog* is a smaller unit, a phrase which serves as the subject of that clause. Other phrases, however, could have taken its place. We could have said *A small terrier bit the mail carrier* or *Something bit the mail carrier,* and so on. The whole range of possible actors in this relationship to the verb phrase (*bit*) and to the object (*mail carrier*) makes up a class of replaceable forms. This class *plus* its functional role in relationship to the rest of the clause can be treated as a tagmeme particle called "subject-as-actor"; *the mail carrier* would be an instance of (or represent) a different functional unit, an object of the clause, as *bit* would be an instance of the transitive predicate tagmeme. (The class sequence noun-verb-noun [N V N] by itself is not enough to represent the structure of the clause, since it does not specify the actor-action-undergoer role relationships of its parts.)

Noun classes may themselves be viewed as particles, however, of a kind different from constructions, relational parts of a construction, or separate words.

Often we have expectations of a form which is under way, long before the form is fully visible. This may be true, for example, of a limerick (see fig. 3.3) even if we hear only the first line. In *There was a young lady from Clyde,* the stresses on *was, lady,* and *Clyde* start a phonological pattern which may alert us to something coming. The choice of the words *there* and *young* contributes to our beginning expectation. The grammatical structure of *was* after *there* adds a further clue, as does the choice of *lady*—or some analogous noun. By the time we add the second line *Who ate some green apples and died,* we are probably quite certain, now, that we are headed into a limerick. The rhyming of *Clyde* with *died,* the rhythm, and the lugubrious flavor, all encourage this guess.

There wás a young làdy from Clýde
Who áte some green àpples and díed.
The ápples ferménted
Insíde the laménted
And made cíder insíde her insídes.
( / sá'dər ʊnsá'dər ʊnsá'dz / )

*Figure 3.3. A limerick is not a random sequence of sentences, but a single internally complex coherent unit, a "high-level" particle. (Source unknown.)*

The expectation of limerick form leads us to hope for some kind of difficulty which is solved only in the last line by a surprise verbal twist. In this limerick, the pleasure is heightened by the pun of *cider* with *(in)side'er*. No such expectation of form, and delight in finding it, could occur unless the limerick as a whole were some kind of particle, a unity.

Once the hearer (or creator) of the unit grasps the fact that a particular kind of unit has begun, the unit's general pattern itself takes over and demands its formal completion. One is driven by the form once the form is begun and recognized. Language is a pattern of such particles on many interlocking hierarchical levels.

### 3.3. Particles in Linear and Spatial Order

The analysis of some phase of life as made up of a *string* of particles may be called a *linear* kind of order. The mind is able to understand life, in part, by thinking of it as one thing after another. These linear distributions have a great grasp on us.

Learning a different order of alphabet, for example, is not easy. Learning to count also takes considerable effort. In many languages of the world counting has never been developed. In some languages of New Guinea, for example, people (until recently, at least—I myself met some in 1949) count: *one thing, two things, many things*, and then must stop; one man translated his counting system into Pidgin English for me as *one fellow, two fellow, plenty fellow*. In eastern Peru I met, years ago, the man who had invented the number *eight* for the language Piro.

Linear order may be replaced (or accompanied) by items arranged in two-dimensional or *three-dimensional space*. Books may be scattered on a table; flowers may be arranged in a garden; rooms may be divided into upstairs and downstairs floor plans. Sounds can be charted in rows and columns which show characteristics which they share. (The sound /p/ shares with /b/ and /m/ the fact that the lips are closed when it is made.)

Such spatially ordered arrays represent particles as being within a *field*. The linear order of particles and their ordering in a field are both important to linguistics.

# Wave

## 4.1. The Merging of Sounds in Sequence

When one tries to read a paragraph as if it were made up of completely separate particles of sound, an astonishing result is heard. The material is very jerky and practically unintelligible. It is worth trying in order to hear the effect (see fig. 4.A). Natural speech *never* sounds like that. Why not, if speech is made up of particles of sound? Surely the analysis of speech into separate chunks is in *some* manner false—a model useful for some purposes, awkward for others.

The same material will sound very different if, instead of putting spaces between the sounds, one reads the lines very, very slowly indeed—as if a phonograph record were slowed down to half speed—and lets one's mouth movements glide slowly from one sound into another. This also is well worth trying for its effect in comparison to what one would expect if sounds were separate particles. They drift into one another—have no clear starting and stopping points.

Instruments show that the sounds do in fact slur into one another. One sound is not finished before the next one is begun. Speech is more like sloppy cursive handwriting in this respect than it is like printing. The difference between *bee* and *boo*, for example, can be seen by looking in the mirror—lips are rounded for the /b/ of *boo* while they are getting ready for the following vowel.

Words may be so run together that they become completely or partially simultaneous (see fig. 4.2). Some years ago my teenage son used to pro-

A. O-l-d-M-o-th-e-r-H-u-bb-a-r-d-w-e-n-t-t-o-th-e-c-u-pb-oar-d

B.  *old mother hubbard went to the*

Figure 4.1. Sounds smear together in natural speech. If each sound is artificially separated by a pause (A), speech becomes jerky and unintelligible. If one reads B equally slowly (like a phonograph at half speed), one can see in a mirror the continuously changing mouth positions.

A. *I don't wánt to.*
B. [ã-ĩ-õ-ã́-n-ə̃]

Figure 4.2. Words can merge. The word not (A) has already weakened to n't. A whining child may merge this much farther—almost into a sequence of nasalized vowels (B). (Pronounce the schwa [ə] as the vowel in cup. The tilde [~] means the air comes out the nose at the same time, to make nasalized vowels.)

nounce the phrase *I don't know* (along with a shrug of the shoulders) using just the sound m, with a hum which rises, then falls considerably, and rises a little bit. If we hear something like that in a foreign language, it may sound incredible (see fig. 4.3). In Chinantec a similar smearing of m over a couple of syllables has led to some verbs where the entire conjugation is given with the mouth closed. (Most of us do a bit of this kind of thing in məm for English 'no', and mhm for 'yes'.)

A. (English)   m⎤⎣_   'I dón't know'

B. (Chinantec) m⎤⌐   'I ask for'

m⎤⌐   'He asks for'

m⎤ ɂm   'You [singular] ask for'

m⎤· m⎤ɂm   'We [I and he] ask for'

m⎤· mɂ   'You [plural] ask for'

m⎤·⎤ɂ   'We [I and you] ask for'

*Figure 4.3. Smearing of sounds can be carried to such lengths that only a hum, with pitch, is left. In English the sentence* I don't know *may become* m *(A); a line drawn over the letters shows the English emic scale of four relative pitch levels: just above the letter, high; just below, mid; extra high and low may also occur. (One may whistle the pitches to get a crude idea of the pronunciation.) In Chinatec (B) of Mexico, there are also four significant pitches, but as regular parts of ordinary words. (Perhaps an old stem vowel has smeared into the* m, *and then the* m *has smeared over onto the suffix. The dot represents extra length; the [ɂ] is a glottal stop, as in the middle of a sharply pronounced* Oh oh!*) (Data from Robbins 1961.)*

## 4.2. Nucleus and Margin of Wave

The clearest or steadiest part of a sound during slow pronunciation can be called the *nucleus* of a *wave*. The borders, or transitions, from one sound to another can be called the *margins*. In wave types which interest us we often look for their nuclei and margins. If our attention is almost exclusively on the nucleus, however, we may be thinking in terms of particles. When our attention is on the whole flowing movement from margin to nucleus to margin, we are thinking in terms of the unit as a wave.

Human nature requires that people *focus* attention in some direction—on some element or concept or view. The person who tries to watch construction out of the corner of his eye while he drives down the road is likely to end in the ditch. Language reflects this capacity for directing focus. Stressed pronunciation can be used to emphasize or highlight parts of a sentence, as in *I said THEY must go!* So can grammar, as in *It is indeed the CAT that swallowed the RAT* where the phrase *it is indeed* forces a focus on CAT. If the two kinds of attention crisscross, we may call the phonological one emphasis (*the RAT*) and the other focus (*It is indeed the cat*). When whole paragraphs are involved, the focused nuclear beginning sentence may be called a *topic*.

## 4.3. Types of Wave

Even when no special attention is called for, the dynamics of behavior organizes speech and action into wave units with nuclei and margins.

We may call a *grammar wave* one in which there is a central, crucial, nuclear part of a construction which may or may not be preceded or followed by less important elements which in some way modify it. When such a wave is made up of just one word, the nucleus may be called a *stem*, and the margin a *prefix* or a *suffix* as in *inactive* or in *singing*. A two-word phrase, smaller than a clause, may also have its head and modifier, as in *my* (margin) *alligator* (nucleus). When two clauses are in a sentence, one may be independent, nuclear, and the other dependent, as in *The doctor treated the boy* (nucleus) *after he broke his leg on a skate board* (margin). Similarly, a question-answer relation gives a higher level of nucleus-margin: *Will you come? Perhaps.*

A *phonological* wave can be as short as a single sound or as large as a lecture. Each may have nucleus and margins. In figure 4.1B, the drawled pronunciation allows one to hear the slow (premargin) approach to the center (nucleus) of the separate sounds, and the slow postmargin, a departure from that central part. In figure 4.3, the entire sentence *I don't want to* is a single, larger phonological wave. The *I don't* is premargin, *to* is postmargin, and *want* is the stressed syllable making up the nucleus of the stress-group wave. The smearing of the English words, in such a situation, is often the result of pronouncing the premarginal section very fast. The nucleus is usually pronounced more slowly, and is less likely to be lost or changed.

A *referential wave* shows highlighting of reported events, or of argument, or exposition. Thus a story can be viewed as a wave: a premargin may set the stage; the plot warms up; the climax (the nucleus) occurs; the hero gets out of trouble and lives happily ever after (postmargin). For a very special kind of story wave, see figure 4.4.

The use of waves in analysis does not eliminate need for the use of particles. Even a wave, when it is viewed as a unit, may itself be treated as a particle, just as the particle, when viewed in its physical smearing aspects, can be viewed as a wave.

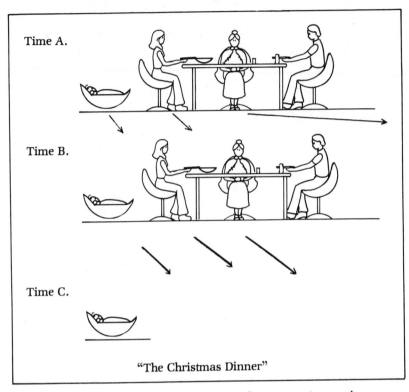

*Figure 4.4. A play as a standing wave may focus attention on the un-
changing role-structure of a family with a grandmother as premargin,
parents as nucleus, a child as postmargin. These roles and their inter-
relations can be kept constant while different generations grow into and
out of these roles. In Wilder (1963), a scene at a Christmas dinner is kept
constant, while some ninety years pass as a wave: baby in basket turns
into mother sitting at the table; mother gradually drifts into the slot of
grandmother; old ones die and drift off stage.*

A pebble dropped into a pond sends out a wave in all directions from the
center. So also, a word may comprise *a lexical wave* with a *central meaning* normal to the most frequent or nonspecial set of contexts and a set of
marginal meanings which occur when the central meaning is modifed by
other words in the context. For example, *to run* is basically (in my *intuition*) referring to the action of a man (or creature) in his feet moving
rapidly toward or away from some place; but *a run in a stocking*, or *to
run the business*, or *to run into trouble*, or *He ran out of words* are margi-

nal. In such instances, we may also sometimes speak of the nuclear meaning as *normal,* and the marginal one as *off-norm.* Slang, or idioms, may therefore be treated as off-norm, relative to the usage of the community as a whole, or frequency of usage, or some criterion of appropriateness as seen by the community.

An item prominent in a general setting, or in a painting, can be viewed for some purposes as an instance of a perceptual wave, with focus on the item or figure as nucleus and on the setting as marginal.

A wave view can even be used to characterize the sweep of scientific history. The nuclei of a science over time would be periods of relative stability in its presuppositions, methodology, and objectives. Kuhn (1962) would call such a nucleus the "continuation of a research tradition," or "normal science" (11), or a "paradigm" (23) of a theory (ix). The prenucleus of such a wave for him could be called "the genesis" or emergence (ix) of a new theory as it gains its status (23). The postnucleus of one of these waves would be seen when researchers notice, among other things, "the insufficiency of methodological directives, by themselves, to dictate a unique substantive conclusion to many sorts of scientific questions" (3). Kuhn's own focus, however, might be said to aim at a discussion not of nucleus, postmargin, or premargin, but at the juncture *in between* the waves, the "transition" (xi) moment itself, or the "extraordinary episodes" which "are the tradition-shattering complements to the tradition-bound activity of normal science" (6).

# 5

## Field

We have discussed the way in which elements can be viewed by themselves as particles, or as waves smearing into some kind of continuum whose prominent parts make up nuclei. Now we turn to sets of relationships which occur when units are linked to one another by their presence in some larger system. A total set of relationships and of units in these relationships we call a field.

### 5.1. Unit Determined by Relationship to Context

No item by itself has significance. A unit becomes relevant only in relation to a context. Outside such a relationship the item will be necessarily uninterpretable by the observer. A simple circle, for example, may be interpreted by an observer as a numeral, if it is in the context of the number *1,000*. On the other hand the circle may be interpreted as a letter of the alphabet in the context *pop*—or as eyes, nose, or teeth, or buttons, or a wheel, in a picture (see fig. 5.1). When, therefore, one asks what *is* the circle in one of these circumstances, it seems clear that its *"factness" is relative to the observer*.

The observer interprets data relative to context—within a field. In this sense a datum of sensation "becomes" a "fact" of human significance when seen relative to its distribution in an environment—relative to a field as structured in the perception or imagination of some person.

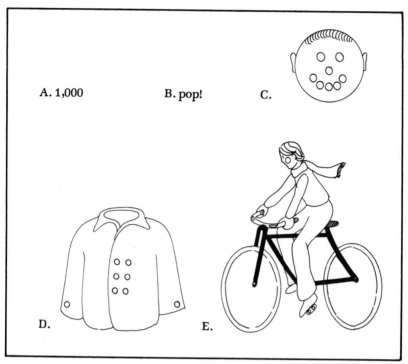

Figure 5.1. Units determined by their relationships to context. A circle is perceived as a talked-about fact only in relation to a field and to an observer of that field.

## 5.2. Sounds in Dimensional Patterns

Symbols representing phonological units of a system can be placed in rows, such that each sound represented has at least one feature (or component, property, characteristic) in common; units in a column also share a feature (see fig. 5.2A). If the symbols for the sounds are removed but the presence of features is shown by arrows (see fig. 5.2B), a circle around the place formerly occupied by a consonant symbol contains a point of intersection of two of the arrows. Either the unit can be treated as merely a "point" at the intersection of features of a field, or the presence of the units can be treated as setting up the field by the relations between them. This kind of display allows us to show that several (intersecting) characteristics are *simultaneously* present. In this simple diagram, only

A.

| | With lips closed | With tongue tip closing the mouth | With mouth closed at the soft palate |
|---|---|---|---|
| Stopped air stream without vocal cord vibration | p | t | k |
| With vocal cord vibration | b | d | g |
| Air escaping from the nose | m | n | n |

B.

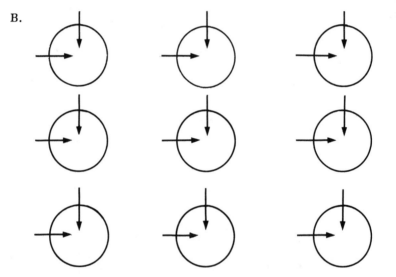

*Figure 5.2. A phonological field seen as a pattern of sounds with features which intersect (A) and as a set of points at the intersection of features (B).*

two dimensions are suggested as relevant—but in principle a field of characteristics can be specified.

A vowel system, like a consonantal one, may be viewed as a field. If we mark the highest point of the tongue on the "pictures" of /i, a, u/ we can use these points as a crude basis for a three-by-three diagram in which /i/ and /u/ are in the top row, in front and back columns, with /a/ in the lower row, middle column. The implied field structure can be used to describe other vowel sounds as well (see fig. 5.3). X-ray pictures by various scholars have shown this scheme to be not completely accurate, but the general scheme continues to be useful on a practical phonetic basis, as an approximation of the way the sounds can be heard in "perceptual" space.

In baby talk the setting of the grid may as a whole be moved higher in the mouth, with the result that a smaller part of the mouth cavity is used. When all of speech is thus transformed, it sounds as if it were coming from the small mouth cavity of a child. If, on the other hand, the whole vowel triangle is pushed farther front, the general effect may be more like Spanish.

Further dimensions than high versus low and front versus back can also enter into the articulatory field. Work (for example, Stewart 1967, Pike 1967*b*) on African languages has emphasized that the movement of the root of the tongue in the throat opening may serve as a further more or less independent dimension. When the root of the tongue is pushed front, leaving the top of the tongue more or less unchanged (see fig. 5.4A), a rather hollow quality may result from the greater openness of the throat cavity. A whole set of sounds in many languages of West Africa may be affected by such a movement. The closest American English equivalent might be the difference between the vowel quality of the word *feet* versus that of *fit* (/i/ versus /ɪ/); of *boot* versus *put* (/u/ versus /ʊ/); of *cape* versus *kept* (/e/ versus /ɛ/). Figure 5.4B shows how the vowel chart can be shown with a third dimension, tongue root position, to suggest this. A simpler chart can be given by subdividing rows to show this difference (fig. 5.4C).

## 5.3. Clauses in Dimensional Patterns

In tagmemic theory we have attempted to develop the use of charts to show the field structure of clauses (Pike 1962, Pike and Pike 1977:140–43, 236–37) just as charts have been used for centuries for phonology; each row (or column) indicates a feature shared by that row (or column). One subset of the clauses of Spanish can be shown in figure 5.5A; their abstracted features occur in rows and columns. A feature of independence contrasts with dependence: *Les hacen traversuras* 'They do tricks to them'; versus *porque hacen la presentacion a base de estudio de casos* 'because they base their presentation on the study of cases'. A feature of intransitivity (without object allowed) contrasts with transitivity (with object required), and with an equational feature: *Hablé con el dueño del café* 'I spoke to the owner of the cafe' (intransitive, without direct object); *Les hacen travesuras* 'They do tricks to them' (transitive, with 'tricks' as direct

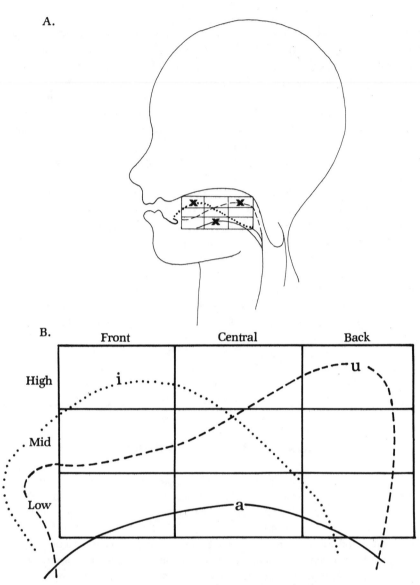

*Figure 5.3. The highest point of the tongue can be used to set up points on a grid. Vowels can then be described, crudely, in reference to such a scheme. In A, the grid is seen superimposed on the mouth. In B, it is abstracted and labeled. The plan is pedagogically useful. Physical details must be modified and refined by presentation of X-ray studies.*

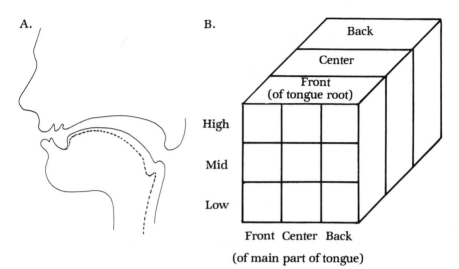

A.

B.

Back

Center

Front
(of tongue root)

High

Mid

Low

Front Center Back

(of main part of tongue)

C.

|  |  | Front | Center | Back |
|---|---|---|---|---|
| High | Root front | i |  | u |
|  | Root back | ʟ |  | ∪ |
| Mid | Root front | e |  | o |
|  | Root back | ɛ |  | ɔ |
| Low | Root front |  |  |  |
|  | Root back |  | a |  |

*Figure 5.4. The root of the tongue, pushed front, opens the throat and sometimes gives a hollow quality to a sound (dotted line in A). Backing the tongue in the throat may choke the vowels or consonants. This characteristic can be shown by a third dimension of a field display (B), or by subdividing rows of a two-dimensional display (C).*

A.

|  | Transitive | Intransitive | Equative |
|---|---|---|---|
| Independent | Independent Transitive | Independent Intransitive | Independent Equative |
| Dependent | Dependent Transitive | Dependent Intransitive | Dependent Equative |

B.

|  | Primary (Basic) | | | Secondary (Derived) | | |
|---|---|---|---|---|---|---|
|  | Transitive | Intransitive | Equative | Passive | Impersonal | Descriptive |
| Independent |  |  |  |  |  |  |
| Dependent |  |  |  |  |  |  |

*Figure 5.5. Dimensional matrix of Spanish clauses. The units may themselves be presented, with certain features important to their contrasts, labeled A; or an extra dimension (here, primary versus secondary—that is, basic versus derived) may be presented as some kind of subdivision of a two-dimensional display (B, after Brend 1968).*

object); *Eso fué el regreso de Ocotlán para acá* 'That was the return from Ocotlán to here' (equative).

Various added dimensions of contrast can be handled either in three-dimensional display or as a subdivided two-dimensional one (fig. 5.5B).

## 5.4. A Poem as a Field Structure

It is intriguing, also, to study much larger units than the sentence in reference to field structure. Suppose, for example, that we take Robert Browning's poem "Memorabilia" (see 1895, and fig. 5.6). One could choose to interpret the poem as representing a kind of field of miscellaneous particles within the memory. Within this field two happenings are described: The first deals with Browning's meeting of a man who met Shelley. The shock of this caused Browning to pale, since even such an indirect contact with the great man Shelley was staggering. The second event deals with the finding of a feather. In some sense each event seems to be perceived as abstracted from experience, as if without relationship to time before or after. Therefore they seem strange, because unchanging, and so somehow eternally new, like some carved figure frozen on a Grecian urn. Art and emotion share these characteristics. I well remember, myself, when a friend, after taking his three-month-old baby to the hospital for

## A. Memorabilia

Ah, did you once see Shelley plain,
    And did he stop and speak to you,
And did you speak to him again?
    How strange it seems and new!

But you were living before that,
    And also you are living after;
And the memory I started at—
    My starting moves your laughter!

I crossed a moor, with a name of its own
    And a certain use in the world no doubt,
Yet a hand's-breadth of it shines alone
    'Mid the blank miles round about:

For there I picked up on the heather,
    And there I put inside my breast
A moulted feather, an eagle-feather!
    Well, I forget the rest.

                      Robert Browning

## B. Field-Memory

|  | Particle | Wave |
|---|---|---|
| Event I: Meeting a man who met Shelley | I | II |
| Event II: Finding a feather | IV | III |

*Figure 5.6. Large units may show field structure. The Roman numerals in the cells (B) represent the stanzas of the poem (A) by Browning. As particles (I, IV) the events seem isolated and unchanging, therefore strange and new. As waves (II, III) the events are known to have been tied to a before and an after, with movement and integration into the real world as a whole. (From Pike 1965:291.)*

emergency brain surgery, said, "As the elevator door closed behind the cot with my child on it, time stood still." The picture congealed.

Under appropriate circumstances, the same event can be viewed as particle, or as wave, or as field—or as a combination of the three, with one more prominent than the other in the perception of speaker or of hearer. A person's emotional state or his immediate or remote experience affects his conscious or unconscious choice of priorities to be given to one of the three. And his language often reveals this choice.

## 5.5. Verbal Cues

Verbal cues that an observer has chosen to adopt (partially at least) a field view may often be seen through his use of words or phrases such as pattern, structure, arrangement, blueprint, plan, network, system, relationship. Some words can be grouped together in sets of threes, suggesting (for me) particle, wave, and field respectively:

    static, dynamic, relational
    item, process, relation
    point, line, space
    list, rule, pattern
    identifying, making, organizing
    abstraction, fusion, intersection
    repetition, change, integration

But there is an analytical awkwardness about observer reality here: at any particular moment there can be an overlap or an indeterminacy among his perspectives. Whereas an observer is sometimes likely (in my judgment) to think of a particular unit as a particle, he may at other times find himself thinking of the same unit as changing in a wavelike fashion, and at still other times as a point in a contextual field within which it gets its meaning.

An observer may shift his attention from an item to its background, thereby treating the background as a whole as itself a unit. One may note, from an airplane at night, the wave character of moving or changing lights in a city below, then focus on the general pattern of arrangement of the lights, and then change once more to admire the city as a whole. Focus has shifted from wave to field to particle perspective. Or one can combine them, by saying, "Note the beautiful changing pattern of lights of that city as a whole."

# II

## The Unit

# Introduction to Part II

In Part I, we talked about ways in which we can look at things or experience: The world can be viewed as if it were made up of particles, of waves, or of field. Perspective has been the focus of our attention, with analytical focus itself coming under focused attention. In Part II we go over much of the same ground, but with the observer in the background and the observed data themselves in the foreground.

Chapter 6 tells us how we can recognize a unit when we find it. This is important. If we could not recognize units—things, people, actions—how could we live as social human beings? Chapter 7 discusses the fact that a unit may be found or perceived in a variety of forms. Chapter 8 shows that a unit to be significant must be appropriate to certain times, places, or situations.

# 6

## Contrast and Identification

### 6.1. Recognition via Contrast and Similarity, within Field

Recognition of a unit involves a curious difficulty: We do not know what something is unless we know something about what it is *not*. Recognition is, in part, negative. In part, it deals with the contrast between units, rather than with the identification of isolated units. One does not know what a horse is if he cannot tell it from a cow. One does not know Susie James if one cannot tell her from Susie Pennyfeather (see figure 6.1).

The same components which help us to see that one unit differs from another also help us to *recognize* the unit when it is no longer close to the one which we separated it from. If, for example, we treat *seal* and *zeal* as two different words, with the /s/ and /z/ being two different sounds as components of the two words, then we can use either /s/ or /z/ to recognize words where they do *not* pair up in contrasts—as *zebra* is clearly recognizable even when no *\*sebra* can be found (with the asterisk before the word meaning that no such instance is known). Features which are contrastive in relation to some contexts are *identificational* in others.

When we go around trying to find units, we could get useless answers if we were to ask only "What is X *not* like?" If we want to know, for example, what a door is, we hardly feel enlightened if we are told only that it is neither a star nor a pebble nor a skunk. A component of a contrast seems to be interesting only if we feel that somehow the two units being contrasted are *similar*. Random contrasts, without reference to similarity, interest us only

*Figure 6.1. Contrastive components which have served to* differentiate *pairs of units can serve also to* identify *them when apart from one another.*

occasionally (as, for example, when we want to talk about randomness it-self—comparing cabbages, kings, and pebbles).

But what do we mean by similar? Units will appear to be similar only if they share some component within the same universe of discourse. Joey and Billy of Seattle can be compared easily, since they share maleness, youth, and the same community. Concepts of contrast and similarity, then, circle back on the concepts of field and observer interest.

## 6.2. Matching for Contrast

Many of the most interesting problems of contrast and dif-ference occur when the items to be compared are very similar indeed. Oc-casionally, for example, my wife has wanted me to buy her a spool of thread. Until she has given me close instructions, it has turned out cata-strophically; thread color and cloth color did not match. She taught me to take along a slip of cloth, but comparing spool with cloth still would not serve. She instructed me to unwrap a bit of the thread, put it on the cloth, and hold it in natural light, moving it around a little bit; then, and only then, I began to get the kind of match she needed. Colors can be told apart better when they are matched side by side in proximity—even, one might say, in the same tiny, temporary "universe of discourse" of color and light and setting.

Similar considerations apply to sound. We hear differences best when we hear them in a near identical context. Good procedure for phonological analysis encourages us to listen to the respective sounds in contexts that are as much alike as possible. Often this means in word pairs which are otherwise identical (as *seal* and *zeal*, which are called *minimal pairs* because the difference is restricted to the sounds (/s/ and /z/) under attention). In Mazatec, for example, there are words which differ by the presence or absence of a difficult-to-hear /h/ before or after the consonant, as in *tho* 'gun,' -*hto* 'rotten,' or its absence in *to* 'fish' (I omit the tones).

The beginner's ear may play tricks on him and refuse to listen at all, and "tell" him that the words sound the same. Under such circumstances, it is very helpful if the meaning is different. The human being learns most easily to pick up contrasts between elements which are highly significant to him. If, for example, two similar words are such that one is obscene and the other is not, it is astonishing how much faster he learns to hear the relevant contrast of sound than he does if he has no social problem growing out of error.

Here again there is an observer component in linguistics. Seeing or hearing or learning is facilitated when the observer has a stake in the outcome. We are born to talk with meanings; we are not built to talk only nonsense. Even our analytical equipment works best when these conditions are taken into account. Language is not merely a set of unrelated sounds, clauses, rules, and meanings; it is a total coherent system of these integrating with each other, and with behavior, context, universe of discourse, and observer perspective. It is a *form-meaning composite* (see Chapter 12). Units can contrast in their respective forms, in their meanings, or in both.

In studying an unknown language, the linguist must crack its code. He must find and learn to recognize and use the units of speech which allow the native speaker to understand and be understood, to act and to react appropriately; he must learn to recognize and utilize units from an *insider's* view.

When such units are sounds of a certain language system, they are called *phonemes*; each of them is *phonemic* in relation to that particular language. Generalizing from phonemics, I coined the term *emic* in 1954 (Pike

1967*a*: chap. 2) to represent any such unit of language, from any level of any hierarchy (see below, chapters 9–11), or from any nonverbal system. (Variants of emic units will be discussed in Chapter 7.)

## 6.3. Contrast in Contextual Frames

If we think of the different possibilities of pronunciation of the third syllable in figure 6.2 as different gates through which the speaker can walk, then we can think of the process of speaking as the process of picking one's way by some path through one gate after another. In figure 6.2, the path goes through mid (tone 2) in the first syllable, then through high (1), through high again in the third syllable, neutral (3), low (4), mid (2). But in the third syllable the alternate *potential* choices which were *not* taken are shown as dotted, leaving the actual chosen path as a solid line. When the full set of choices is in fact available, the analyst can compare the contrastive levels of the tones of these items of the substitution set with each other as well as with that of the high frame tone of the second syllable (for this technology, see Pike 1948).

The choices of the substitution list are *independent* of one another (any one of them can be chosen at that place); they are relevantly *different* from one another (they contrast with each other at that place and may—or may

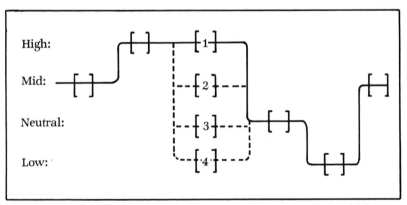

*Figure 6.2. A frame technique chooses a sentence or phrase in which words can be successively replaced in one slot. The number of alternate contrastive pitch paths in the substitution slot often represents the potential of the tone system at that point. A high, unchanging frame tone is especially useful. (From Pike 1952, fig. 6.)*

not—make a difference of meaning when used); they are *consistently* different in this context (there is no haphazard—free—variation between them at this point such that one overlaps in pronunciation with another). That is, they are *emically different.*

The lack of variability would seem obvious in a situation involving gates through fences. But in the use of pitches of the voice, that is not true. So we

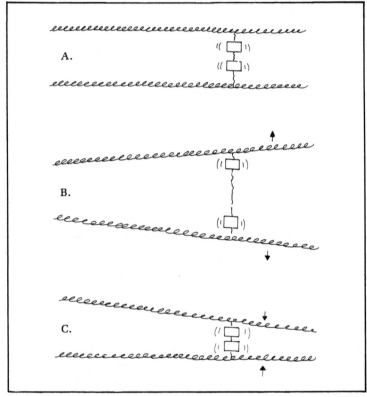

*Figure 6.3. Tones may have variants conditioned by mood of the speaker. Let us suppose that we have two tones, represented as weights suspended between springs (A). When a person speaks emphatically, the tones may be farther apart (B); a quiet or phlegmatic mood (C) may move the tones closer together. In addition they may jiggle a bit, in* free *variation around a norm. (From Pike 1952, fig. 1.)*

use a supplementary illustration (fig. 6.3) of variation of tone (anticipating more theoretical discussion of variation in Chapter 7). Under excitement, the whole frame-cum-tone may be raised; or its tones may be stretched further apart (fig. 6.3B); or in hushed speech around a camp fire they may be substantially lowered (fig. 6.3C). Yet in each such instance, they may continue to be consistently different from one another.

(Other problems, not under attention here, may give further headaches to the analyst: different consonants or vowels or a different number or kind of syllables of the words of the list may also cause changes; and lexical replacements in the frame itself may cause sharp differences of *replacement—morphophonemic changes*—of one emic tone by another in words on either side of it. An unrecognized replacement of a tone of the frame itself, furthermore, may cause errors concerning the perceived pitch of the words of the list. As a partial defense against unrecognized but disruptive changes, one is well advised [especially in languages of Latin America] to seek for a frame in which some one of its tones is always as high as or higher than any word of the substitution list. In this circumstance, any word of the list which is at the same level as that high frame tone can itself be considered emically high.)

In figure 6.4A is given a list of utterances from the Mazatec of Huautla, Mexico, in which 'causative' is *si*¹; in 6.4B 'to place, or to repeat, or to place repeatedly' is *vᴐe*¹; in 6.4C 'continuative' is *ti*¹. In each of these groups the substitution list contains words with the respective tones from 1 to 4. By putting all of the sets together, one can see that there is a random relation of the consonants starting the words of the substitution list, so that those consonants do not destroy the tone contrast (by implying that the pitch difference is conditioned by the consonant). The pitch contrasts are therefore *independently, consistently different*—that is, *emically contrastive*.

Consonants—and vowels—may be similarly contrasted with one another in frames. Usually, however, there is less variability in their pronunciation growing out of moods or other contexts.

## 6.4. Contrast Seen via Matrices

We have already seen that sounds can be lined up in charts, or matrices (figs. 5.2A, 5.4C). These show the relation more than with just one sound, or than with one set of sounds in a particular frame. Rather, they line up the contrasts of a *subsystem* of sounds—which may *itself* be treated as an emic unit. A three-dimensional matrix of sounds has been seen in figure 5.4B. These charts may be labeled as component-times-component displays (that is, with components labeling the rows and the columns). The component-times-component presentation was used again in figure 5.5, but for a display of some Spanish clauses rather than for sounds.

Other kinds of matrices may show advantageously other features of a system; among these is a display of units as columns, components as rows, and an indication of a component's presence (by a plus sign) or absence (by a minus sign) in the cells. In figure 6.5 a still different type of matrix is shown for a display of clause types as rows, the naming of *classes* of tagmemes as columns, but the naming of the *particular* tagmeme of that class in the appropriate cell. For Zapotec, of Mexico (Pickett 1960:35), this helps

**A1.** si$^1$ hnti$^1$          '[he] makes [something] dirty'
si$^1$ši$^2$          '[he] makes it dry'
si$^1$ški$^3$          '[he] gives medicine to'
si$^1$ški$^4$          '[he] counts'

**A2.** si$^1$he$^1$          '[he] asks for'
si$^1$te$^2$          '[he] makes [something] dance'
si$^1$he$^3$          '[he] fattens up [something]'
si$^1$kao$^4$          '[he] touches'
si$^1$ɔya$^4$          '[he] makes string'

**A3.** si$^1$ša$^1$          '[he] works'
si$^1$jnta$^2$          '[he] borrows'
si$^1$ča$^3$          '[he] looses'
si$^1$kao$^4$          '[he] touches'

**B.** vɔe$^1$čhi$^1$          '[he] pays'
vɔe$^1$ši$^2$          '[he] dries [something]'
vɔe$^1$thi$^3$          '[he] spins [something]'
vɔe$^1$ški$^4$          '[he] counts'

**C.** ti$^1$nčha$^4$ntɂe$^1$          '[he] is talking persuasively'
ti$^1$nčha$^4$nthai$^2$          '[he] is talking in defense of'
ti$^1$nčha$^4$to$^3$          '[he] is speaking as he passes by'
ti$^1$nčha$^4$kao$^4$          '[he] is talking with'

*Figure 6.4. Tone contrast in frames may help in the analysis of the number of emic tone levels. A high frame which is high and unchanging in some contexts, as in the Mazatec of Huautla, Mexico, allows for recognition of contrast (data from Eunice V. Pike 1958:95–165).*

**Zapotec**

| | Predicate tagmeme | Dependent subject | Independent subject | Object | Personal referent |
|---|---|---|---|---|---|
| Intransitive declarative | + IntrDeclPred | + DepS | ± IndS | — | — |
| Transitive declarative | + TranDeclPred | + DepS | ± IndS | + 0 | — |
| Personal referent declarative | + PRefDeclPred | + DepS | ± IndS | + 0 | ± PRef |

*Figure 6.5. A unit-times-component matrix for clauses of Zapotec (Mexico). Each clause differs from each of the others by a difference in the predicate. There is also the obligatory presence or absence of object, and optional presence or obligatory absence of personal referent.*

to show the contrastive structure of the clause types, in terms of labeled elements in the sequence in which they occur in their respective clauses. Notice, in this figure, that there is an obligatory predicate for each, but that each predicate is different from the others, and that there is the obligatory occurrence of an object in the second and third rows, but with an optional referent in the third only.

## 6.5. Contrast in Verbal Meaning and in Behavior

We have illustrated contrast between sounds and contrast between clauses. Contrasts between meanings of lexical units can also be seen through matrix displays. For words-in-cells (comparable to the sounds-in-cells in fig. 5.2), note figure 6.6, where the components male versus female, and royal persons (reigning versus nonreigning) versus animal are abstracted from the data in the cells and used to label the rows and columns of the matrix.

Sometimes words are pronounced alike, but have different meanings. The contrast between their meanings sometimes is clear because of the different contexts in which the words with these particular meanings are allowed to occur. The word *big* has several lexical meanings which are not

|  | | Male | Female |
|---|---|---|---|
| Royal | Reigning | king | queen |
|  | Nonreigning | prince | princess |
| Animal | | tiger | tigress |

*Figure 6.6. Matrices can display meanings of lexicon, with units arranged and labeled according to shared features.*

|  | big X | X is big | How big is X?, or X is very big, or X is bigger. |
|---|---|---|---|
| $big_1$ | a $big_1$ rock | The rock is $big_1$. | How $big_2$ is the rock? |
| $big_2$ | my $big_2$ sister | *My sister is $big_2$. | *How $big_2$ is my sister? |
| $big_3$ | a $big_3$ fool | *The fool is $big_3$. | How $big_3$ a fool is he? |

*Figure 6.7. Words may have contrastive senses. The word* big *can refer to physical size (1), to elder relation (2), or to the degree to which a characteristic is present (3). Inappropriate usages are marked with asterisks. (The matrix is adapted from Lamb 1964:74.)*

easy for the beginner to differentiate. If we try to use the word *big* in various different contexts, however, they fit some of the contexts correctly, but not others. One may say *It's a big rock*, or *The rock is big*, or *Is the rock very big?*, or *How big is the rock?*, or *The rock is bigger*. But in the sense *big* of *my big sister*, one cannot say *My sister is bigger* or *How big is my sister?* In figure 6.7 these differences are shown in a matrix.

It is not only in language, however, that contrast is relevant to meaning, purpose, or culture. A person, in English, may signal *Good-bye!* by waving the hand downward several times. (Spanish speakers sometimes misinterpret the English gesture as meaning *come*.) To signal the contrastive meaning *come* in English, one is likely to turn the palm of the hand upward, and move the index finger upward and inward.

This pair of English gestures is part of a whole set of gestures (culturally conditioned manners of eating, sitting, or even smiling) which make up another universe of discourse with its contrastive features, varying according to language or geographical area. Some years ago in Australia, for example, I amused myself by trying to tell, by looking at advertisements in the locally published journals, whether or not the photographs were taken of

Australian girls or of American girls. Often I could be quite sure. In those instances, the smiles were radically different; American girls smiled with the corners of the mouth a bit open, whereas the Australian girls frequently smiled with the corners of the lips closed. When I called this to the attention of the Australians, one of them replied, "Yes, those American pictures look like toothpaste advertisements!"

# Variation

Normal social behavior requires that we be able to recognize identities in spite of change. Unless we can do so, there can be no human society as we know it (see fig. 7.1, and compare fig. 2.7).

## 7.1. Referential Identity in Spite of Change

The problem of identity within change is not new. Heraclitus said: "Into the same river we both step and do not step. We both are and are not" (fragment 81, in Patrick 1889). Or one may fail to find identity at all: "Into the same river you could not step twice, for other [and still other] waters are flowing" (fragment 41). If the river is made up of molecules of water, then—since the molecules have changed—you can never bathe in the same river again; the molecules will have flowed by you.

In this chapter we are especially interested in those features of a unit which may change *without causing the loss of recognizability* of the unit. The appropriate observer readily recognizes that certain changes do not affect deeper identities.

The pattern as a whole can change subtly and gradually over a period of time. The child grows into a man (compare fig. 2.7). From stage to stage of growth and change the parents have no difficulty recognizing him. But for me a picture of a child a few months old may in some instances not be at all distinguishable from that of his brother when he was the same age.

The outside analyst—an observer alien to a native system—may have a great deal of difficulty in determining precisely those features which are

**Yesterday**          **Today**

*He:* I can't take you to the party.
*She:* Why not?
*He:* You're not the same girl I promised—you're wearing
your hair in a bun!

*Figure 7.1. Refusal to acknowledge identity within variability would stop
all normal behavior.*

diagnostic for recognizing minimum structurally and behaviorally relevant
segments of sound (phonemes) which to the native speaker—the inside observer—are reacted to as in some way unchanged entities. Nor can the outside analyst expect that the native actor can tell him what the specific cues
are which allow him to recognize the unit.

How well I remember once when my own boy, at about six years of age,
was lost for a time. Ditches were being dug all around our dormitory to put
in telephone lines. Dusk came, police were called, a search was made.
"What does he look like?" "Well, he's tow-headed, has a dimple in his chin,
and was last seen wearing a pair of overalls." Since he had no outstanding
physical characteristics, it was impossible for us, his own parents, to give a
description which was very helpful. Changeable bits (the overalls) were
included along with more permanent components (his light-colored hair—
which, however, has darkened in the years since then). The *overall* pattern, including many unanalyzed bits, carried the total signal of identity—
for his parents—in some kind of known field patterns beyond words.

Even persistent obvious cues have a range of change. There is *no* set of unchanging, *precisely* same, distinctive components in any language, or across languages. The analyst may act—falsely—on the assumption that once enough cues have been identified to differentiate sounds, these alone are the cues actually used by the native speaker. But the speaker has—and uses—more cues than he needs in an idealized context. Some variable ones are redundant from the viewpoint of minimum descriptive elegance, but important to communication—under noisy conditions, for example. The analyst may desire a succinct, traditional logical definition which aims to limit the data in a definition to a *minimum* set of criteria which will place a unit in a taxonomic classification. This kind of definition refers (*a*) to elements which differentiate a unit from similar units, and (*b*) to elements which place it in a taxonomic hierarchy: for example, a chair differs from a table, but both belong to the class *furniture*. Tagmemic definition—or description, if one prefers the term—differs from classical definition by insisting on the inclusion of further defining characteristics: (*c*) the *range of variability* of an item, as treated in this chapter, plus (*d*) the *appropriate* range of *occurrence* of a unit as it is distributed in system (or field) rather than merely its distribution in class or sequence (see chapters 5, 8, and 14).

## 7.2. Changes in Pronunciation

In listening to his own English, the beginner, furthermore, may find this chapter difficult to understand or to follow, precisely because he doesn't notice the changes in his own native speech. From this point of view one can say that he is reacting to the structure of his own language as if it were a kind of model or theory in which (most of the time) he leaves out wisely any major attention to minor variants (see discussion of models in section 1.2). If he were constantly focusing attention on details irrelevant to signaling contrastively the normal meaning or purpose of behavior, he would never be able to concentrate on the crucial intent of its messages. Yet at the same time—and in a paradoxical relation to the variants—he must be able at any moment to pick up cues from minor characteristics of units if the major components get lost or covered (as under noise). In addition, the variants can simultaneously be *crucial signals of style*, or attitude, which are important from a social viewpoint. If, for example, Joe says to Sue, "That's a beautiful hat you've got on!," but says it with a contemptuous growl, she will understand the deprecative meaning as overriding the (opposite) lexical one.

Variation can affect not only the pronunciation of the individual phonemes, but can lead to addition, replacement, or deletion of some of the sounds in the words—that is, to *morphophonemic* changes. The command *Come here!* may become *C'm'ere!* in some rapid speech. Many American speakers whom I have checked pronounce *Ed had edited it* as /ɛdɛdédɛdɛdʊt/ (with /ɛ/ the vowel of *dead*, /ʊ/ the vowel of *bit*, provided they pronounce the sentence fast, without pause, and with stress only on the third syllable). Yet because of the morphophonemic changes, the sentence pronounced in isolation is often unintelligible to these same speakers. Context (universe of discourse, field) is relevant to the set of mind within which understanding takes place. In part, one hears what one expects to hear. In another kind of morphophonemics words may *share* sounds, as /ž/ may be shared by *as you* in rapid pronunciation.

## 7.3. Changes in Grammar

Units of grammar may have free or conditioned variants just as can phonemes and morphemes. Free variation in the *manifestation* of the subject of a clause tagmeme can be seen in the replacement of one word by another in the same slot. In *The tiger swallowed the boy* and *The snake swallowed the boy*, both *the tiger* and *the snake* fill the subject slot. Since the grammatical relationship in these instances is the same, the change is a kind of *free* variation.

*Conditioned* variation can be seen in the predicate: Compare *The tiger sees the canary* with *The tigers see the canary*. The change from *The tiger* to *the tigers* forces the change from *sees* to *see;* the free change from a singular to a plural subject forces a conditioned change from singular to plural predicate. That is, the presence of a freely chosen plural variant of subject tagmeme conditions the presence of the plural variant of the predicate.

Variation can also affect the placement of parts of grammatical constructions (for example, in clauses). The word *yesterday* can either precede or follow *I came from Detroit.* Viewed more or less in isolation, the placement of the time tagmeme is free to occur either early or late in the clause. In a paragraph context, there are instances in which having it early gives it prominence, or *focus.* That is, the placement choice is *locally free,* but *focus-* or *style-* or *discourse-*conditioned. Compare the sentence *I came from Chicago today but yesterday I came from Detroit* with *I came from Chicago today but I came from Detroit yesterday.* Compare also *He gave me the book* with *He gave the book to me* (but not, comfortably, *\*He gave the great big book I used to own in Ann Arbor to me,* since we prefer to have the long element at the end).

Constructions sometimes have *abbreviated* variants also: *She can sing better than I can sing,* or *She can sing better than I can,* or *She can sing better than I.* There are also restrictions in the utilization of particular lexical items with particular grammatical ones. Here the lexical and grammatical systems affect one another. We can say *You know the way,* or *Thou knowest the way* (in elevated poetry or prayer) but not the mixture *\*You knowest the way.* The appropriate occurrence of units involves the whole pattern of a language—not merely its isolated bits.

Sometimes it is convenient to view a subsection of a field structure as itself a single unit which can have variants. In figure 7.2A a matrix is given showing certain of the subject suffixes of some Fore (New Guinea) verbs (from Pike 1963:8–10). No clear set of simple particles can be found which signal the meanings for singular and plural, although the composite forms with first and second person are clearly different from each other. Thus /w/ is *singular* with first person and plural with second person, whereas /n/ is plural with first person, but singular with second person. If, now, to the words containing forms in figure 7.2A a further suffix /n/ meaning 'emphasis' has been added, every form of figure 7.2A changes radically into the form seen in 7.2B. Yet the *same pattern* of crisscross is retained. For some purposes it is useful to say that the *entire pattern* (or field) has been conditioned by the /n/, rather than set up *separate rules* for each separate item or part. (At some other times, when the separate parts need to be in view, an alternate description may be preferred. In tagmemic theory, a field view of conditioning does *not exclude* a particle view of the same data for a different purpose.)

It would be convenient to have some one term which refers to variants of all kinds of units (both phonological and grammatical). A solution is to call a variant of any emic unit an *allo-unit* (from a Greek work meaning 'other'). Thus we can have allophones of phonemes; allomorphs of morphemes, allomatrices, and so on.

| A. | First | Second | B. | First | Second |
|---|---|---|---|---|---|
| Singular | (u)w | (aa)n | Singular | (o) # | (aa)mpe |
| Plural | (u)n | (aa)w | Plural | (o)mpe | (aa) # |

*Figure 7.2. Conditioned variants of a field structure can be seen in Fore (New Guinea) subject suffixes. A crisscross occurring between /w/ and /n/ in A is paralleled by crisscrossing zero (#) and /mpe/ in B. The change from A as a whole to B occurs before an emphatic suffix /n/.*

## 7.4. Indeterminate Segmentation

We have implied that the separation of segments in a sequence is at times difficult since a small element which lies between two larger units can be partially or completely shared by each of them when they are partly fused (see fig. 4.2 and *as you* in section 7.2). In such circumstances a person can know *that* two units are present in a word even though he may not know *where* the two units respectively end and begin. Sometimes, that is, segmentation is *indeterminate*—as can be seen in the following illustration.

Myra Barnard and Janette Forster, members of the Summer Institute of Linguistics, were working as a research team in a remote aboriginal village, where the planes of the institute shipped them supplies. It became awkward to keep the accounts (as in dividing up charges for a half kilo of carrots to each member of the pair) every time a joint shipment was sent. The finance office, therefore, encouraged these girls (and other pairs of field linguists) to adopt fused names. The Barnard-Forster combine was called *Barnster* (see fig. 7.3A).

At their staging center, furthermore, each pair shared a mailbox; and pairs often got social invitations addressed to the name combine. One day I was invited to lunch with Barnster. Mary Jane Gardner also happened to be living in their house, sharing part of their center expenses but not their tribal expenses. To the three of them there was now applied a triply fused name: *Garnster*. I asked them to tell me which part of the name belonged to which girl. With *Barnster* it appeared easy. *Barn-* represented *Barnard*; *-ster* represented *Forster*. This would represent a simple particle view, with obvious unambiguous breaks between the parts; this kind of segmentation allows the parts to be easily identified and entered into a dictionary or morpheme listings.

But with *Garnster*, many difficulties arose. Gardner claimed the *Garn-* as all her own—providing a particle segmentation, to be sure, but leaving poor Barnard as a zero feature (#), unmanifested (as in 7.3C1). Barnard protested—so Gardner allowed her to claim *simultaneously* the *-n-* (C2); this shared *-n-* would represent the border fusion in wave view. But Barnard still revolted, demanding instead that *-arn-* be all hers, with Gardner being left only with *G-* —from a particle view, but with a different segmentation (B, C3), perhaps a compromise there would have been C4 or even C5. Thus far, each of these (apart from zero and fusion) preserves the contiguity of the parts. In C6, however, Forster is robbed of her *-er* by the grasping of Gardner who adds it discontinuously to her earlier-in-the-word

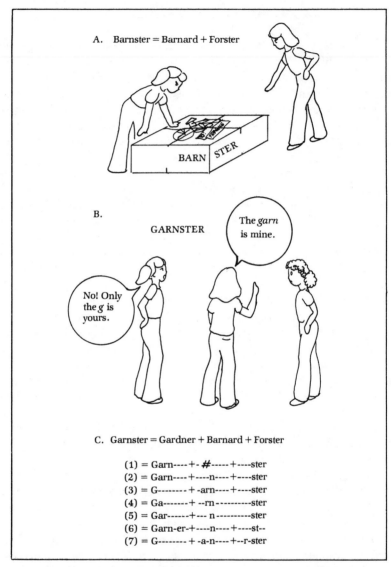

*Figure 7.3. Segmentation may be indeterminate even when the presence of units is certain. In a remote village a pair of girls shared transportation services (A), and a joint fused name for the bill. Elsewhere a third girl (B) joined the combine. Alternate possible segmentations of the fused name (C) point up the fact that variation brought on by fusion may lead to arbitrariness of segmentation. (From Pike 1964:85.)*

material. In reverse, C7 transfers the -*r*- of the first syllable analytically (*not* in pronunciation) over to Forster.

A *particle* view demands segmentation, even if it be arbitrary, acting *as if* it were possible to make a clean-cut segmentation even when in fact it is not. A *wave* view asserts the presence of units, without needing specific identification of border points (or arbitrary pretense of such points) for its kind of description of the fused unit-as-a-whole. When variation arises from fusion of segments, treatment by the two perspectives differs radically: choice between the two depends on the varying needs of the analyst. It is the observer perspective or judgment, not the data, which is variable here.

# 8

## Distribution

### 8.1. Distribution of Units as Relevant to Their Identity

Some place must be the point of origin for the coordinates which allow one to identify oneself in a place in the larger world. Something must tell us where we are, beyond reference to our immediate environment. Reference to successively larger patterns of occurrence, to a larger *universe of discourse,* is necessary if one is to know the significance of a person, a thing, or a word. Knowing that I'm behind my nose does not tell me how to find the way to town. I need to be oriented in reference to a larger context, to a universe—or to a discourse. The *I* of a discourse (in relation to *you*) suggests that the speaker knows something about his social relations. But unless one goes beyond oneself and his neighbor to a hierarchically ordered outside world, he is in some sense lost within himself.

Even the schoolboy senses this, and can get excited when it dawns on him that he fits a slot in a larger structured world. How well I remember sitting at a desk in a one-room red brick schoolhouse, when I was in the third grade. I wrote out my address as being "Woodstock, Connecticut, USA, World." I received a second stage of pleasure many years later when I had called to my attention that Joyce (1968:15) said of one of his characters, "He turned to the flyleaf of the geography and read what he had written there: himself, his name, and where he was" (see our fig. 8.1).

The same problem of identity and belonging affects adults who are just becoming aware of a larger world beyond their province. Some years ago I was talking with teachers in a very remote nook of the world, where the

*Figure 8.1. The school boy relishes an address (Joyce's Portrait of the Artist as a Young Man) which places him in a context. Seeing himself thus distributed into the world, his self-awareness is given sharper focus.*

students had traveled no more than a few miles in their entire lives. Yet the teachers had to prepare them for life in a world of threatening war and of United Nations debate. Only a few months were available beyond the fifth grade to get the students ready to teach others. What could then be said to help them understand their place in the world? Perhaps:

> *See how the brook winds down through this little valley? Now you go over the mountain. There is another valley*—(Yes, we know that—one of our uncles wandered over there once and was killed.) *Well, if you go into another valley, and another one, and another one, you come to some water with salt in it. There you may see a house that floats and you can push with a motor.* (Oh, like the one we hear in the airplane going overhead.) *After the house swims that way as far as you have walked, then as much again, as many times as there are days in a moon, you come to another place where there are people and valleys. That is just the beginning. . . .*

And so on. In teaching the isolated, they had to teach about distribution. Knowledge of identity includes knowledge of relevant distribution.

## 8.2. As a Member of a Substitution Class

A unit, whether a person or word, is in part characterized by its membership in a class of replaceable units which may appropriately occur in the same place(s) in a particular kind of structure. The set comprises a *distribution class* of units. For example, *kitten, dog, train, bicycle* are members of a (sub)class of nouns which can appropriately substitute one for another as head of a noun phrase; compare the phrase *a large kitten* with *a large dog, a large train, a large bicycle*. These phrases, as wholes, are themselves members of a higher-level class of such phrase units which may occur appropriately in the object slot of an English transitive clause such as *Joe saw a large kitten*. (For tones in a substitution list in a frame, see fig. 6.4.)

## 8.3. As Part of a Structural Sequence

A word or the class of words of which it is a member is in part, therefore, characterized or identified by the structured *sequences* (*grammatical constructions, syntactic units*) of which it is a part. That is, a unit is in part defined by the constructions in which it occurs, in addition to the class of items of which it is an appropriate substitute member within such structured sequences. The nouns just listed are in part recognized by the fact that they can occur in a noun phrase, preceded in that phrase by an article (*the kitten*), or an adjective (*the lovely kitten*), or followed by a modifying phrase (*the kitten I used to own*).

Similarly, a person, like a word in a grammatical construction, has a place in a particular social structure which in part identifies him by providing for him certain social roles—say as a son of an elderly father and also simultaneously as father of his own young children, or as the head of the house. In turn, he himself comprises part of that larger kinship structure, just as the noun phrase does not exist without words.

In pronunciation, also, the place where sounds may occur in a sequence of sounds is important in specifying one of the crucial characteristics of that sound. For /h/, in English, it is not enough to say that the air comes out of the mouth without appreciable friction at any one point, without the vocal cords vibrating and with the passage to the nasal cavity closed. It is also

A. *English:* /glɪmpst strimz/ from [He] *glimpst streams* [*in the valley below*]; but not */mpststrop/ as a single word.

B. *Seri (Mexico):* /kaafšx/ 'to go fast', and /ptkamn/ 'lobster', but not: */ptkaafšx/; /kiaai/ 'to cost', but not: */kiaaoeoap/.

*Figure 8.2. Various constraints limit the appropriateness of the occurrence of a consonant or vowel in types of sequences. English has /mpststr/ (A), crossing the word barrier, but the sequence does not occur at the beginning of English words. In Seri (Mexico, based on Moser and Moser 1965) one can have large consonant clusters (or large vowel clusters) (B), but not both together in a single word. (If we assign a value of two to each vowel, and one to each consonant, no syllable adds up to more than ten or so units of value.)*

important to specify that the /h/ may come at the beginning of words but not at the end of them. For the -*ng* of *hang* the reverse is true. One can be startled to see how queer it sounds to pronounce *hang* backwards (as *ng-a-h*). Often it is as difficult to pronounce familiar sounds in strange environments as it is to pronounce strange sounds in any environment. Spanish speakers have a difficult time with words like *school*; they do not have a consonant cluster of /s/ plus /k/ at the beginning of words. They may pronounce the word with a distortion, putting a vowel before the /s/, that is, *eschool* /eskul/.

Each language has its own built-in limits to the number of vowels or consonants it can have together. English can have a monster like /mpststr/—but only crossing a border between words, and not at their beginning (see figure 8.2).

Whenever, in phonology or in grammar, two languages differ in the distribution of their sounds or tagmemes, the speaker of the one may find it awkward to acquire the structure of the other. Problems of language learning can be expected where differences of distribution of otherwise similar units are found. The beginner needs drills to teach him not only new sounds but old sounds in new combinations. This is another way of saying that he *doesn't really know a sound until he knows its distribution* and can control it *in all slots appropriate to it* in a particular language.

Various kinds of elements control the distribution of behavioral units. Linguistic controls, for example, may involve lexical, phonological, grammatical, or referential elements—including style, or coherence within a social universe of discourse. The cluster *shm* /šm/, for example, occurs in English only in special lexical items like *schmoo*.

Grammatical control of the structure of consonant clusters can be seen in that certain of them occur only across morpheme boundaries in which particular lexical items are involved. Note /ks-θ-s/, of *sixths,* in which the numeral morpheme followed by the ordinal suffix *-th* and the plural *-s* lead to the large cluster.

Certain exclamations like *Tsk!,* on the other hand, may be restricted to occasions which are socially defined. (This particular sound which is only vaguely implied by this spelling of it, may be called a *click.* It is made by closing off both the front and back parts of the mouth with the tongue, lowering the mid part of the tongue a bit to make a partial vacuum, and releasing the tongue tip to allow the air to rush in with a hiss or a pop. It may be used informally to express lugubrious disapproval.)

Differences of distribution of grammatical units are as crucial to their definition as are distributional constraints to the specification of emic units of sound. If we have the sentences *Why did you come?* and *Joe is coming today,* how can we know that they represent different syntactic structures? One difference is that this question has an interrogative slot for *why.* Another is the meaning difference—the fact that one inquires, whereas the other states. But a third, important, difference is the class of responses which can appropriately come after each of them (see fig. 8.3). After *Why did you come?,* one does not expect to hear *So I see;* but that might be appropriate after *Joe came today.* Such *contrastive distribution of grammatical constructions in larger constructions*—here in dialogue—can serve as one of the *criteria for identifying them as emically different.* Until one knows the appropriate distribution of constructions, one cannot talk a language well; one does not know where to put words, clauses, sentences—or paragraphs or conversations.

| **Utterance** | **Response** |
|---|---|
| A. *Question:* Why did you come? | *Answer:* Oh—just because.<br>*Or:* He told me to.<br>*Not:* *Yes. |
| B. *Statement:* John is coming today. | *Reply:* Oh?<br>*Or:* I believe you.<br>*Not:* *Oh—just because. |

*Figure 8.3. The contrasting distribution of sentences in larger conversational or narrative structures may help differentiate and define them as emically contrastive.*

## 8.4. As a Point in a System

One can in part define a unit by the place it fills in a matrix of units (an n-dimensional system of units). For sounds in such a display of a system, see figures 5.2–6; for tone, figure 6.3. For affixes in a matrix, see figure 7.2; for word meanings, figure 6.6; for clauses, figures 5.5, 6.5; for stanzas of a poem, figure 5.6. The labeling of the rows and columns of such a display (fig. 5.2A) tells us something of the characteristics of the units listed there.

But their place in a matrix can also be used as a further kind of feature which can help identify and contrast units. If in our preliminary analysis of a strange language we have minimal pairs to contrast sharply all but one pair of sounds in a phonetic chart, lesser evidence in connection with this systemic data may justify the conclusion that the remaining pair is emically contrastive also. In English, one finds *pie* / *buy*, *tie* / *die*, *choke* / *joke*, *fie* / *vie*, *seal* / *zeal*—but not *ship* / *\*zhip*. One does, however, have *mission vision*, where the first consonant of the word pair also differs, along with /š/ and /ž/; and *rush rouge*, where the vowels differ, along with the final consonants. The strong contrastive pattern of the system as a whole supports the conclusion that the /š/ and /ž/ of *mission* and *vision* are different phonemes.

Grammatical patterns may also need analogy in a matrix to help determine some systemic contrasts. Human nature is such that for verbal or nonverbal systems to be operable at all, they must have *some* symmetry about them. Totally random structures are not serviceable in human interaction; a field structure lies at its heart. This does *not* affirm that no exceptions can occur, nor does it affirm that no irregularities will be found. Rather, it affirms that *some* degree of systematization can be found in every functioning structure. It follows that human nature cannot be described accurately, purely in terms of isolated units of sound, purely in terms of classes of such sounds without reference to system, or in terms of a miscellaneous list of rules for combining them. Nor can mere lists or taxonomies of events, gestures, behavior elements, abstract semantic components, or abstract formal rules of action describe human activity in a way satisfactory to us. Somewhere, to some degree, the distributional relation of a unit to a background system must enter the definition of every unit either as an implicit underlying assumption or as an explicit part of the descriptive mechanism.

# III

**Hierarchy**

# Introduction to Part III

In Part I we emphasized certain characteristics which the observer brings to his study of data. The raw material experienced is in some sense inaccessible to us. The observer enters into the warp and woof of the pattern which he seems to observe and report. His report reflects an input from the combination of his perspectives of particle, wave, and field.

In Part II the observer was less in focus, as units observed in the data became the target of study. Even there, however, the observer intruded with judgments whether two different items were emically the same (separate instances of a particular behavioral structural unit), or whether they were rather noncontrastive etic variants of an emic unit.

Now, in Part III, the emphasis shifts again. Here it centers upon three facets of language behavior and structure which interlock with one another, but are also somewhat (but by no means completely) independent one from another. These structural facets may themselves be called *hierarchies*. In the next three chapters special attention is directed, one chapter each, to the linguistic hierarchies of grammar, phonology, and reference. The linguistic terms and concepts have analogies in nonverbal behavior.

# 9

# Grammatical Hierarchy

## 9.1. A Psychological Constraint on Complexity

The relevant structural inclusion of wheels within wheels, of successive inclusion of parts within a whole, with the whole in its turn becoming one part of a still larger whole, is an important component of our approach. We arrived at and have maintained this emphasis because of our own experience with linguistic data. But it is very helpful to find that in the discipline of psychology there is strong support for a hierarchical view. Miller in a now classical article in 1956 summarized and discussed the evidence. The crucial point: There is a "channel capacity" (86) affecting "the span of immediate memory" which "is limited by the number of items" which he calls "*chunks* of information" (92) or "units or chunks" (93), such as "steps" from letter to word to phrase (93). But—and this is vital to understanding both his approach and ours—"The span of memory seems to be almost independent of the number of bits per chunk" in the areas studied (93). And: "Our language is tremendously useful for re-packaging material into a few chunks rich in information" (95); and the limit of chunks per larger chunk seems to be "the magical number seven, plus or minus two" (note his title). But it needs emphasis that this number is that of the chunks—the sections, words, phrases, clauses—*not* the "bits," that is, *not the contrastive features* of the chunks.

Figure 9.1 gives an illustration of the fact that we can recognize at once, without counting, the number of dots which are present when there are only a very few, but that we cannot do the same when there are many. If the

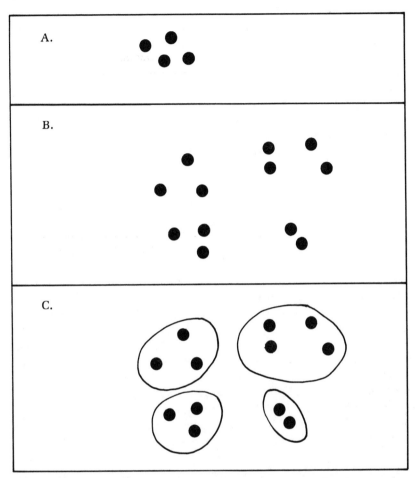

Figure 9.1. Recognitions of chunks is limited by their number (approximately seven) rather than by the number of simultaneous features leading to their internal complexity. In A one can easily see four dots, without counting. In B one cannot tell at a glance what the number of dots is, whereas in C one can immediately recognize that there are four groups of dots (cf. Miller 1956).

dots are grouped, however, we can once more recognize the number of the groups, without counting them, if these too are few (see Miller 1956:90). Similarly, we can easily hear three words in *three big cats* even though it is impossible for us to note quickly where and how many phonological features are present (voicing, various relevant tongue positions, friction, stoppage of the air stream, and others).

## 9.2. Behavioral and Hence Semantic Relevance of Levels of Grammatical Structure

But a "level" of a hierarchy in our view of grammar is much *more* than the mere *degree* of inclusiveness in successively larger chunks. Each major type of level has some *kind of function* in behavior. Its structural arrangement, its form, has simultaneously a general kind of impact on the hearer (which we can call the *meaning* of that level). We are well acquainted with the fact that *s-k-u-n-k*, is a spelling form (reflecting its pronunciation form), but that this is not all; it carries the meaning of a native American animal which puts out an incredibly repulsive odor. The term derives from an Algonquian word (from which the name *Chicago* also is said to have been derived).

Note, for example, a difference between *That skunk smells bad* and *that bad-smelling skunk;* the first formally *asserts* that a state is true; the second merely *labels* the characteristic to refer to it without putting it in the form of deliberate affirmation. The first might start conversation (once *Hellos* are out of the way), but the second would not normally do so. (We say "normally," here, without repeating it in every other relevant instance, since imaginative students or poets can almost always find *some* context— an off-norm situation—where an unexpected form might actually show up. Norms are important to include in a theory at some point; in tagmemics they enter in relation to a wave view.) And the meaningful affirmation characteristic, with various modifications according to context (norm or off-norm), we can call *proposition,* for our purposes; the meaning of the label level we will call *term.*

But we drew upon the concept of conversation in order to reach this conclusion. That is, the *relative independence,* or *relative isolatability,* of propositions is definable only in relation to a still higher level, that of conversation. And this conversation level includes a meaning function of *social interchange.* It is this factor which then becomes our entrance point into many of our linguistic definitions. Language is a part of behavior. It is not isolated from nonverbal action, but is integrated with it, and takes its meaning from social settings, intents, and reactions.

In between the levels of social interaction and of proposition we may wish to posit another: *theme development*. We all know that a lecture is (normally expected to be) more than a sentence; but few of us would care to call it a conversation. Rather, it often takes a topic, in the form of a proposition, and then makes comments about it. A paragraph can do that. So can a lecture on a larger scale, as a single continuous "speech" (except in off-norm situations when, for example, the presumed continuous speech is interrupted by heckling comments from a hostile audience or by *Amens* from some religious ones).

## 9.3. Pairs of Etic or Emic Hierarchical Levels Sharing Behavioral Impact

And now we can generalize a bit more. It is useful to have a preliminary, generalized (etic) view of pairs of types of levels around the world before checking to see whether any one language has them all (it may not), all of them behaviorally relevant (emic) to it, or whether it adds more or lacks some. At the top, the social interaction pair can include both a single dialogue exchange between two people or a conversation between various people. Comparably, the theme-development pair—a bit lower in the hierarchy—can include a paragraph or a monologue (with numerous kinds of disjunctively defined variants not important to us here). Propositions—still lower—can be in the form of clause or of sentence. Terms can be in the form of word or of phrase.

Morphemes and morpheme clusters in words comprise a still further pair of levels—the lowest one in our treatment of the grammatical structure. A *root* such as *berry* would be the simple member of the pair; *blackberry* would be a morpheme complex (here, a compound stem) in *blackberries;* the *-s* 'plural' would be another simple morpheme, an *affix*. In each pair type, that is, there can be smaller (minimum) or longer (expanded) kinds of specific levels within the general kind of level.

A caution: If one wishes them to reflect behavior-as-it-is-lived, definitions often cannot usefully be made as simple or as clean-cut as one might think that they ought to be. Some definitions need to be disjunct—that is, almost a sum of several different definitions leading to a kind of emically defined behavioral impact. Others can be conjunct—that is, a single rule. In tennis, for example, a game is won not by a single, definable kind of physical action, but by a person. Any tennis player—even a very young one—knows that there are several different ways (by disjunct definition) to win a game: by serving four winning points in a row without the opponent getting any; or by eventually getting at least four, but also at least two more than the opponent, without having allowed him to get more than two ahead after the first three; or by winning by default if for some reason the officials rule that the game is validly won whereas the opponent does not in fact play—or finish playing—the scheduled game. The attempt to describe *winning* is not simple.

Similarly, the definition of *sentence* has given great difficulty, in past generations, to persons looking for a single-faceted (*conjunct*) definition in which one descriptive claim fits all the varied instances. But in our approach the sentence is disjunctively defined. As a start, it first is given a subdefinition as a minimal kind of proposition which may start a conversation after the *Hellos*—although this is also one definition of an independent clause such as *Look at that skunk over there!* (which is simultaneously sentence and independent clause in that environment). But as a second subdefinition a sentence may have two or more clauses in it, one of which, for example, is marginal and the other nuclear (note the wave view entering the description), as in *If you want to be careful, watch out for that skunk over there!* For some important purposes, a sentence may have a third subdefinition, which reflects a total response no longer than these others mentioned, but also shorter ones: A word is a response sentence in [*Who is coming today?* Response:] *Lancelot*; but not in [*What did you see today?* Response:] *A big smelly skunk!* When *Lancelot* stood alone, in the first of these two responses, it was *simultaneously* a word and a sentence; when it is included in a longer response, it is still a word but *not* a sentence. That is, the definitions of sentence, clause, phrase, word, and morpheme interlock—overlap—in relation to this occurrence at different times and places in discourse (for details see Pike and Pike 1977). In addition, we have to call on the concept of norm lest we get forced into treating *gl-* in *glance, glitter, glow, gloom* as a morpheme comparable to *skunk*.

A further caution: Sometimes we mention paragraph, word, and the like as if, for example, *a* word *comprises* such a level. But when we speak a bit more carefully, we say that an etic level is made up of a *set* of such elements—for example, all the words of a language together make up the etic level of word.

A third caution: If the researcher into the structure of a specific language decides that there is no emic contrast—say, between etic word and etic phrase—but just the emic level of term, then the set of all etic words and phrases would comprise just one emic level in that language.

## 9.4. The Unit-in-Context (the Tagmeme)

The four features of a tagmeme are *in part independently variable;* they are also mutually dependent on each other, with interlocking components and definitions. In general, these four components help answer questions well known to everyone: (1) *Where* (in what *slot*) in the *immediate* structural setting does some concrete part occur? (2) *What set* (*class*) of units can be parts of that larger containing unit, in that same place in the unit? (3) *Why* is any member of that set of units *relevant* (*meaningful*) to the sets of units in other slots at that same immediately-in-view structure? (4) *How* does the *generalized frame of reference*, on this or other levels of the hierarchy, *reflect or exercise control* (*give cohesion*) to tie the parts together? We shall now discuss these again, in more detail (see also the four-cell diagram in fig. 9.2).

| (1) **Slot** | (2) **Class(es)** |
|---|---|
| Where (the position) | What (the items) |
| Specific place of part in whole | General set of items substitutable appropriately in the slot |
| Wave characteristic, with nuclear or marginal relation | Particle characteristic |
| Syntagmatic relations | Paradigmatic relations |
| (3) **Role** | (4) **Cohesion** |
| Why (the relevance) | How tied to other units |
| Specific function of the set to other sets in the including whole | General background materials from any level of the hierarchy which are controlled by or controlling the item in view |
| Behavioral meaning | Field characteristic, systemic structure |
| Pragmatic relations | Framework relations |

*Figure 9.2. The unit-in-context (the tagmeme) has interlocking features, each quasi-independent, but each dependent on all of the others. Hence the unit in view here is not the isolated lexical item, but a set of elements and features of elements mutually relevant—hence the term unit-in-context. (See notation throughout Pike and Pike 1977, and display 12.3.)*

(1) *Structural slots:* Hierarchical grammatical structures are characterized by parts making up wholes, which in turn make up other larger entities. But for a *general* entity to be recognizable as emically the same, with etic variation involving substituted parts, those parts must somehow be seen as occurring within constant structural positions.

These slots frequently differ as to nuclear versus marginal relations to the structure as a whole. These relations can occur at all levels of the hierarchy: Within the word *skunks* there is a nuclear root (with role of *item*) and a marginal suffix -*s*. Within the sentence *If I can, I shall certainly give that skunk a wide berth*, the marginal *if* clause (with role of condition) has a nuclear independent clause following it (with role of statement). Within the paragraph *It is good to avoid skunks. They are smelly creatures. Why run the risk of having to bury one's then-forever-unwashable clothing?*, the *It is* sentence is the nucleus, and the *They are* sentence is marginal, followed by further explanation in the form of a rhetorical-question sentence. Within the dialogue exchange

*Abe:* Why can't you use your clothing after meeting a skunk?
*Bill:* Because the smell won't wash out!

there is first a nucleus, followed by dialogue margin.

(2) *Substitution class:* At any point in a grammatical structure we can expect to be able to substitute one of various lexical items for another without affecting the *proportion* (the general, not lexically specific, relationship) between the various kinds of chunks of the unit. Thus, instead of *The skunk lent its X to Y*, one might hear *The man lent his presence to the occasion*, or *A big boy whom I used to know lent his top to a friend*, or *The skunk gave flavor to that incident*. Here *The skunk*, *The man*, and *A big boy whom I used to know* are all members of the substitution class noun phrase, and are *appropriately occurring (distributed)* within that subject position. (Note that each would change the message; that is a different kind of change—a referential one—which will be taken up in Chapter 11. Once more, also, "normal" is in view: some items like -*s* 'plural' are not appropriately replaced by anything else under some conditions; in such instances a class may be limited to a class of one—or to one plus zero.)

(3) *Role:* But the *same* class may have a sharply *different* role from one sentence to another. If I say *I smelled the skunk*, the role of the skunk in the act is quite different from that in *The skunk smelled me*. Who is doing what? In the one case it is I who am doing the smelling; in the other it is the skunk. But in the passive form, *I am smelled by skunk*, I am not doing the smelling, even though I am the subject of the clause. It is this kind of fact which forces a long-known difference between form and function in gram-

matical relations. Specifically, we have insisted from the very first publication on tagmemic theory (Pike 1967a; 1st ed., 1954: sec. 7.6) that there was not just one subject tagmeme (called *grameme* there, but *tagmeme* in the second edition, 1967a), but rather a set of various subject tagmemes, differing by role meaning. Thus there was *subject-as-actor* distinct from the tagmeme *subject-as-goal* (but with "goal," a Bloomfieldian term, referred to as "undergoer" in Pike and Pike 1977, or "patient" in the work of case grammarians such as Fillmore 1968).

There is, furthermore, etic variability in the meaning of such roles: While retaining the *same* kind of grammatical *formal* proportion, the substitution of particular lexical items may change the *message* relation (the *referential* relation) between the parts. For example, in *I killed the stinking skunk to get it out from under the house*, I am there a *voluntary* actor; but in *I smelled that intolerable, unavoidable odor*, then I am an *involuntary* actor. (This attention to etic versus emic differences of role meaning differentiates the Pike and Pike approach sharply from that of some other approaches to case. As a further difference, our approach insists on studying such role relations at *every* level of the grammatical hierarchy, not just on the level of clause.)

(4) *Framework and control (cohesion):* Something has to tie words together in some kind of coherent whole, or talk and the perception of the world revealed by that talk would be a random madhouse. Talk structures must have their parts in internal *systemic agreement*, often marked as such by particular bits. For example, *Skunks are mild, beautiful, and pleasant unless frightened or disturbed* differs from *That skunk is lifting his tail— beware, that's a signal that it is getting ready to be offensive!* The background frame of reference includes number (one versus more), and this is reflected in *Skunks are* versus *That skunk is*, and the words *is* and *are* are selected (controlled by) the number difference of *skunk* versus *skunks*. In addition, *it* is selected because it is controlled by the fact that animals are usually (apart from personification in folk tales or other circumstances) treated as nonhuman and referred to by the neuter pronoun. And the present tense is used both in *are* and *is*, controlled by the grammatical frame of reference which is that of a "telling style" which is talking about more or less permanent characteristics which can be represented by that tense (with the speaker talking now, about the situation now). From language to language, however, the choice of the particular kinds of items to be formally marked for coherence varies (for example, *in sight* versus *out of sight, older* versus *younger, reported by the speaker as known from his experience* versus *reported but with the speaker refusing to take responsibility for its accuracy*).

The contrast between slot, class, role, and cohesion can also be related to

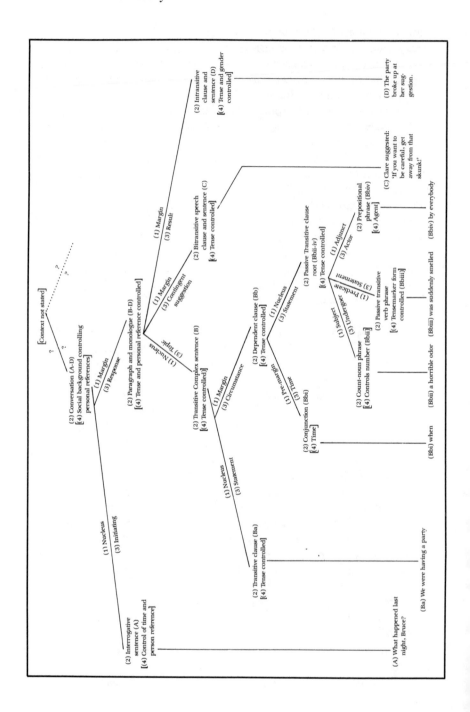

other terms known to linguists: (1) *syntagmatic* relation to a sequence of parts in a larger whole, (2) *paradigmatic* class, of appropriate replaceable parts in a comparable place, (3) *pragmatic* relevance of behavioral function of that kind of chunk, (4) *agreement* of items.

## 9.5. Diagrams and Formulas for Unit-in-Context

For effective work, however, one must be able to apply his general ideas to specific detail. Yet when the detail is enormous in its variety, as in language, the mechanism for representing it is found to be complex. A theory or notation which is too simple may omit crucial behavioral details.

A mathematics without a notation would be less useful than it is with. The change from roman numerals to arabic numerals makes the practice of multiplication different. Practice, as well as theory, changes the world. What kind of notation can help to move us from a view of language as made up of words as isolates (with their inner structure making up the whole of grammar), or sentences as isolates (a view which thinks that there is no grammar beyond the sentence), to a view that *all* units are perceived as relevant *only* in relation to an including context or set of contexts? Or that even language as a whole cannot be isolated "as a separate science" (a dream of some of my teachers) without dependence on items outside it in culture as a whole?

In order to illustrate one kind of tagmemic notation, we give a brief sample in figure 9.3 as a part of the grammatical hierarchical structure of a

---

*Figure 9.3. A tree diagram, tagmemically labeled, can show successive hierarchical inclusion of grammatical constructions as units (as immediate constituents) within a particular larger construction. (1) A slot label on a branch shows its inclusion in a higher unit, for example, as nuclear or marginal to its wave features; (2) beneath the branch a function label shows its role in relation to the including whole; (3) at the point of junction (the node) a construction label gives the name of the part which happens at the moment to be filling the including slot; and (4) along with that construction name there is sometimes given in brackets a suggestion as to controlling or controlled features in relation to other items at the same or at different levels of the including hierarchy or of the system. Because of space limits here, only a sample of the relevant labels are given, and structures inside the verb phrase and noun phrase are omitted as well as details of most of the clauses and sentences.*

single conversation outlined in a way somewhat like a (very old) classical sentence diagram (or *tree* structure), but with the parts labeled by the four-cell tagmemic features. (For more detailed illustration, and for the technology by which one *arrives at* such tagmemic analyses, see Pike and Pike 1977.)

The tree diagram of figure 9.3 splits the sequence of the conversation into its successive immediate constituents. It first suggests, by the dotted line to the upper right, that the conversation is embedded in a situation larger than the conversation itself. At the bottom of the tree, the actual conversation is given, with pairs labeled for reference as A to D. At the top, just at the lower end of the first line slanting to the left, is the number 2, which refers to Cell 2, the class; the name of the class at this point is *conversation*, covering the indicated span from A to D; and immediately below that, in brackets, is a suggestion of its relation to background material or linguistic social system, from the cohesion Cell (4). This sequence then breaks down into two tagmemes, leading to right and left branching lines. The left branch is marked above the line for Cell 1, as *nucleus*, and below that same line for Cell 3, as having the role of *initiating* the conversation; the interrogative sentence comprises the filler of Cell 2 at the lower end of that branch. The right-hand branch is marked as *marginal, and response,* manifested by *paragraph*, in which tense and personal reference are controlled for cohesion.

The paragraph B–D in turn breaks down into a nucleus and two margins which are respectively *topic, contingent suggestion,* and *result,* manifested by a transitive complex sentence (B), a bitransitive speech clause (C) which is here simultaneously a sentence, and an intransitive clause (D) which is here simultaneously a sentence. The complex sentence B is then broken into clauses Ba and Bb; and the passive transitive clause root (Bbii-iv) is broken down into subject, predicate, and adjunct. For lack of space, further breakdown is not given. (But for illustration of bitransitive with tagmemes of subject, predicate, adjunct as undergoer [direct object] and adjunct as scope [indirect object], see Pike and Pike 1977.)

There is much detail in such a figure. Nevertheless, one major gap is present there. It gives only the structure of one particular conversation, or one particular clause or phrase type at a time. It does not show how these are instances of broader recurrent patterns, each with a range of variability involving more or fewer optional tagmemes. In part to fill this gap, we give one sample of a more general formula in figure 9.4. Such a formula represents a large number of *potential* instances built on that pattern. In this sense it simultaneously *represents* (or *generates*) them all.

An English independent declarative bitransitive clause is chosen for representation in that figure, but limited to its root form (omitting modifiers of time phrases and others), and represented by an abbreviated name. Four tagmemes are represented, with three of them obligatory (subject, predicate, adjunct as undergoer [object]), and with one of them as optional (adjunct as scope [indirect object]). The characterizing formula follows the equals sign. Then each tagmeme is given, first with an indication as to its normally required presence (shown by plus—though the tagmeme may be omitted in some special discourse contexts where the context is clear), or as to its optionality (shown by a plus-minus sign). Then comes an abbreviation for the characteristic of the slot (subject, predicate, adjunct), followed after a hyphen by the role feature (actor, statement, undergoer, scope). A colon is then given, following which the class of fillers of the slot is indicated (for example, noun phrase, declarative verb phrase, a noun phrase beginning with *to* or with some comparable particle). In this particular abbreviation no cohesion feature is given. (For discussion of this kind of notation, see Pike and Pike 1977:12–18, 36–37, 39–40, 44–46, 412–54.) In the passive clause root Bbii–iv of figure 9.3, the formula would have to be changed, to make the subject have the role of undergoer instead of actor.

The data are so complex that different scholars have given primary attention to different selections from the data, with different resulting types of formulas. Bloomfield, for example, used the roles (our term, not his) of the tagmemes of a clause root to label the clause. For example, his terms "actor," "action," "goal" (or "undergoer") (1933:267) would represent our actor, statement, and undergoer in a transitive clause root. For Jespersen (1937), on the other hand, the labels were more like those of our slots, as subject-predicate-object. Fries (1952:76–86) chose, for notation, word classes similar to noun and verb, but labeled them with the numbers one and two. A notation based on the cohesion cell could also be invented, I suppose, but I do not recall having seen one; perhaps one could experiment, for the same clause root, with the concept of relation to number, for example, and label the subject-predicate-object as controlling unit, controlled unit, and noncontrolled unit.

But under some circumstances, it is a decided loss if one loses easy reference to different phases of the unit-in-context—circumstances, for example, where the *normal* relation of *role to class* is *overridden*. Note the question directed by a starchy lady at a sniffling youngster: *Little boy, do you have a handkerchief?* To which he replied: *Yes, ma'am, but I'm not allowed to lend it to anybody.* Here the lady's impatient intent (role) was a *command;* but its relation to class was *off-norm* since it was spoken with

## A. An Independent Declarative Bitransitive Clause Root

| | (1) Subject | (2) Proper noun root / Subject pronoun / Count noun phrase | (1) Predicate | (2) Declarative verb phrase of saying |
|---|---|---|---|---|
| + | (3) Actor | (4) Subject controls number of predicate / Nominal controlled by discourse | (3) Statement | (4) Speech bitransitive phrase, with its presence mutually controlling and controlled by the presence of adjunct-as-scope ("indirect object") and subject-as-actor, adjunct-as-undergoer ("object") Number controlled by number of the subject. |
| | (1) Adjunct ("indirect object") | (2) *to* with noun phrase / Location phrase / Location word | (1) Adjunct (or "Object") | (2) Sentence or clause of various types—including statement, interrogative, declarative, imperative, or other / Count noun phrase / Pronoun / [And other, including monologue] |
| ± | (3) Scope (or "indirect object") | (4) Gender and number controlled by discourse setting | (3) Undergoer (or "object" or "goal" or "patient") | (4) Gender and number controlled by discourse |

B. **IndeDeclBTClRt** = +**S-A:NP** +**P-Sta:DeclVP** +**Ad-U:CNP** +**AdSc:toNP** interrogative form (class). The boy, however, interpreted it as if it were a request. (See Pike and Pike 1977:49–50 for a systematic display of further illustrations.) The voice quality which the woman used was probably brusque—and should have signaled its off-norm intent, but the boy missed the signal.

---

*Figure 9.4. A generalized four-cell tagmemic notation. In A the descriptive terms are written out for easy reading by the person unacquainted with the abbreviated symbols. In B a partial summary is given, to show the way the symbols are more likely to be abbreviated when less of the data needs to be in view. This formula represents a clause root such as* Bill gave the skunk to the garbage man *or* Bill gave him the skunk, *with further variation of the order in which the adjunct-as-scope may come in the clause.*

# 10

# The Phonological Hierarchy

We have seen a number of characteristics of units of the phonological hierarchy, anticipated in other contexts. Sounds may smear together (figs. 4.1–3). They enter a field structure (figs. 3.6, 5.2–4). They may carry relevant tone contrasts (figs. 6.4–5). They may be displayed in component-times-unit charts (fig. 5.2). Their place in a word affects the difficulty in pronunciation, and their number and arrangement affect syllable structures (fig. 8.3). Now we focus on the phonological hierarchy per se, instead of using its characteristics incidentally to illustrate other elements or principles.

## 10.1. Noncoterminous Borders of Phonological and Grammatical Hierarchies

In the last chapter we discussed chunks of material arranged into grammatical units. But at the *same time,* the *same substance*—for example, the same sentence—is arranged differently, into phonological chunks. And these segments, like the grammatical ones, are hierarchically ordered—but with their borders sometimes *not* coinciding, and therefore forcing an analysis of the system of language into distinct hierarchies. Thus *skunks* was one syllable but two morphemes (root plus suffix), as well as being one word; but *horrible* was one morpheme (and one word) but three syllables. Similarly, *to be cáreful* is just one stress group (it has just one accent, shown by the acute mark over the vowel), but it contains three words, with four syllables and four morphemes (see fig. 10.1).

*I'm*—Grammatically: Word border occurs between *I* and *am*.
Phonologically: No syllable border occurs within *I'm*.

*Figure 10.1. Noncoterminous units of grammar and phonology are the justification for treating them as distinct hierarchies.*

## 10.2. Relevance Criteria for the Pairing of Levels

In the last chapter we showed that there were behavioral reasons for organizing our description of the successive inclusion of grammatical chunks into pairs of kinds of chunks; there was a social relevance to such a structuring scheme. So, for pronunciation, there are sharp differences in the function of different levels of chunks in the hierarchy. Just as in grammar the clause and sentence have a kind of independence (relative to the other levels) in being able to initiate a conversation (after a *Hello!*), so also there is a kind of *phonological independence* which is more likely to be related to the syllable and to the stress group (a pair like clause and sentence) than it is to an isolated sound (like *k-*) or to a cluster of sounds (like *sk-* or *-nk* in *skunk*) less than the syllable. It is *relatively* simple, in most languages, to teach even a preliterate to pronounce a phrase in terms of syllables, but *very difficult* to have him separate the sounds one at a time. (Note that for the latter I do *not* mean the *names* of the letters as given when a word is spelled, with /w/, for example, named to sound like "double-you.")

Even for professionals in phonetics it takes some concentration to be able to isolate the sounds one after another. So this independence characteristic is important. Given that fact, it is less surprising to learn that writing in terms of syllables has been invented various times in history, but that almost every alphabet—perhaps every one—ever invented has had some kind of remote indebtedness to an accident in history arising in the Middle East which abstracted some signs for an alphabet (at first consonants only) from the hieroglyphs of Egypt. These at first were merely word pictures, of which some twenty-two were later extended in usage to represent any of the syllables whose initial consonant was the same as one of that small subset of the many hieroglyphs. (See Gelb 1963 for a more precise statement of this history. For the pairing of phonological levels, see Tench 1976. And see sec. 10.6 below for consonant clusters.)

## 10.3. Constraints of Focal Attention

But this last section reminds us of figure 9.1, where we saw that the mind inevitably grasps things, features, or subunits by clustering them into units, when the nature of the mind makes it impossible, say, to count or to identify separately all of the included items or features at a glance. So also, here in phonology, a hierarchy of chunks is necessary for our understanding of human behavior.

The *minimum* (shortest) such phonological *chunk* (segment) which meets the requirements laid down in section 6.3 for being *independently, consistently different* from other chunks is the *phoneme*. The articulatory movement toward the nucleus of such a wave of sound (sec. 4.2), or the movement away from that nucleus, can be important and contrastive. This can be seen, for example, if one merely hums the sounds *m, n,* and the sound *-ng* of *song,* without a vowel; they sound much more alike than they seem to us if we speak aloud the words *sum, sun, sung*—where the glide off from the vowels helps to enhance our perception of the contrast. Similarly, the (usually) longer vowel in *cub* may help us to tell the *-b* from the *-p* of *cup,* where the vowel may be shorter. Yet neither the glide away from the *-u* of *sung* nor the glide toward the *-b* of *cub* attains, by itself, the status of a phonemic chunk.

It must be emphasized again, however, that such a relevant sound is an emic chunk, not an etic one: that there are phonetic variants of each such phoneme chunk, depending upon the environment in which the phoneme occurs (as, for example, the /n/ differs slightly after or before *-u-* in *sun* or *numb,* or as it differs slightly before the different vowels of *numb, nymph, neck, noose, nap, know*). Machine recording of such sounds shows up differences very clearly. But the normal (nonphonetician) speaker of English does not *notice* the specific details as such—he cannot talk about them in academic terms or identify verbally the differences—even though he may hear as a queer foreign accent the way foreigners depart from our norms in using them. In the same way we can recognize a friend as the same person when he smiles or frowns, laughs or cries, but we may be unable to describe him (that is, put into words the detail about his face as a chunk) so that he can be picked out in a crowd (unless, that is, he has some *very* strange characteristic such as a nose twisted horribly).

It comes as a shock, therefore—or as incomprehensible and therefore almost incredible at first—to learn that such minute differences can be the basis of word differentiation in some language other than our own. For example, the two *p* sounds of English *paper* are so different, as caused by their position in relation to the stressed first syllable, that the same phonetic difference (the aspiration—the puff of breath—after the first but not after the second) can signal a difference of meanings (such as /tʰi/ 'circle,' versus /ti/ 'it burns') in the Jalapa Mazatec Indian language of Mexico (data from Judy Schram).

## 10.4. Source of the Terms *Emic* and *Etic*

And it was specifically my academic inheritance of this verbalized knowledge from former scholars, plus my own application of it in the analysis of languages hitherto unwritten, which forced me to see that *comparable* situations existed in *all* human behavior. I extended the terms *phonemic* and *phonetic* to behavior as a whole by dropping the *phon-* (implying *pronunciation*), and using only their endings *emic* and *etic*. The tagmeme, as discussed in sections 9.4–5, is one of these units, where the concept (but not the term) was developed in response to my question: Is there a "phoneme" of grammar which will have analogous characteristics of contrast, variation, and relevant distribution (as presented in Chapters 6–8)?

## 10.5. Simultaneous Features— and Where Do You Stop?

I may be unable to describe my friend's face in such a way that others can quickly recognize it, but that is no reason to decide that the physiologist cannot study—and talk about—the function of the eye and its parts, or that the biologist cannot talk about the cells of the eye, or the chemist the molecular structure of a few of its bits, or the physicist the atoms in some of it or the way in which light acts in relation to a lens. A person talks about what he is interested in and about things which he has knowledge of inherited from former scholars or has discovered for himself.

And wherever he stops, there is always the opportunity for someone else to probe in more detail into the hierarchy of the universe as a whole. In phonetics one can wonder how the atoms affect the muscles which drive the tongue to articulate a /t/. Or one can wish one could know the size of the units which control the eardrum, or nerve fibers, or brain components so that one can hear twenty thousand vibrations per second. Yet one must stop arbitrarily, somewhere, knowing that there is no end. My conclusion: *One cannot ever work adequately with a philosophical reductionism which demands that one begin with the smallest bits of the universe,* but must rather adopt the view that each person (and each discipline) *jumps in wherever he pleases and works up and down the hierarchy of reality* until he finds answers to questions tantalizing him, or until he gets tired, or runs out of ability-in-the-face-of-the-current-state-of-the-discipline. People will differ in these judgments and choices.

In this chapter, my attention has thus far ended in its "downward" view by concentration on the minimum chunk, the phoneme. But in section 5.2, and in figures 5.2–4, I was discussing *simultaneous components (features)* of phonemes in relation to their articulatory fields. There was a sharp discontinuity of phoneme to feature because of the possibility of simultaneity of features in a single chunk: The /b/ of *maybe* is made up, in part, of the simultaneous presence of the vibration of the vocal cords (called *voicing*) plus the closure of the lips and of the passage from the back of the throat into the nose. This in part comprises a consonant which has cessation, for the moment, of air coming out the mouth and nose (that is, it is a *stop*).

Many scholars prefer to give much greater prominence to such simultaneities than I do, however. They may treat them with little (if any) discussion of the kinds of problems I have been interested in here. That is, they may try to list a set of features occurring in many languages, but treat them implicitly as if in any one language they were unchanging. This view is inadequate. The *features themselves* must be treated as emic, and as *etically variable*. For example, the English phoneme /b/ by no means always shows up as having clear vibration of the vocal cords throughout its entire pronunciation. Other characteristics, such as the lengthening of a vowel before a word-final /b/, may help to signal its contrast with a word-final /p/ (as in *cub* versus *cup*). These factors of sequence conditioning, with relevant bits carried by adjacent sounds, are not easily accommodated within a set of features theoretically treated as if they were wholly invariant. (A person who wishes an introduction to the feature approach might consult Hyman 1975; in a foreword to it, Victoria A. Fromkin says, "Chapter 2 deals with the basic building blocks of phonology—distinctive features." For further extensive historical introduction to varieties of phonological theory and practice, see Fischer-Jørgensen 1975.)

Going up the hierarchy, like going downwards, also has its difficulties. The handling of tone and stress are related to phonological units larger than the phoneme—that is, to distribution within the syllable, or within a phrase larger than that. But phonology goes still further. A lecture as a whole, for example, may have phonological characteristics as a unit, in that one may sometimes detect when the speaker is running down towards the end, by the characteristics of his voice quality.

## 10.6. Wave Characteristics of Phonological Units

The way we print books makes it easy for us to think of sounds as particles, since the letters in a word are separated by spaces. In longhand writing, the smear between them is more visible orthographically. In pronunciation, the smear and overlap is, however, substantial (as we saw in secs. 4.1–2, with nucleus versus margin illustrated and discussed). Now we add further detail about phonological hierarchy.

*Phone* (a particular variant of a phoneme, from some particular kind of environment): for example, /n/; with a premargin on-glide towards it (as in the glide toward *-n* from the *-u* of *sun*); followed by its nuclear peak (when the closure of the mouth passage is completed by the tongue tip); followed by the postmargin off-glide (as the tongue releases).

*Syllable* (or an etic variation of an emic syllable): with a premargin on-glide to it comprising one consonant (in all languages possible, and in some languages obligatory), or more than one consonant (like *str-* in *strict*); with a nuclear element comprising at least a vowel or a syllabic consonant (the *-i* in *strict* or the *-m-* in the exclamation *hm!*), and sometimes two or more vowels (as in the /aⁱ/ of *strike*, according to the analysis of English adopted here—but as /ay/ in the same word, according to some alternative analyses), or a vowel plus a consonant closely joined with it such as *h* or a glottal stop (the closure of the vocal cords) in some languages; and with a postmargin consonant or group of consonants, in some languages (as *-mpst* of *glimpst*).

*Stress group* as a wave: see section 4.3, with *wánt* as the nucleus of the stress-group wave of *I don't wánt to*, pronounced very fast, smearing the words as in figure 4.3.

*Phonological paragraph:* the nuclear theme material may sometimes be pronounced slowly, distinctly, loudly, and with relatively high pitch, whereas a marginal element, such as an aside (often written in parentheses), may be more rapid, softer, lower in pitch, and perhaps less distinct—or even set off by pauses.

*Phonological discourse:* may comprise a monologue marked somewhat like the paragraph just mentioned, but with the characteristics spread over a large unit. In addition, it may build up to a discourse climax, and at the end taper off phonologically. (If the speaker gives these finalizing signals, but speaks too long and doesn't end there, his audience may comment wryly that he missed several good stopping places.)

*Utterance and response:* voice quality and speed are to some degree likely to be set by the initiating speaker (who is acting in a nuclear phonological role). For example, a question showing urgency and hurry may elicit a more rapid, tense reply (the margin) than would have been received from a quiet question asked in front of a fireplace.

The speaker of English must be prepared for many surprises, however. Instead of something which he might think of as syllables, he will find in some languages that units of length may be important, emically. For example, in the Mixtec of San Miguel el Grande, Mexico, every isolated pronounceable unit must have two length elements. The unit can be made up of two etic syllables (like English syllables), as in *kata* 'to sing'; or it may be composed of just one long etic vowel, after a consonant, as in *ka·* 'will climb' (with a long vowel shown by a raised dot), which must be analyzed as /kaa/ with two emic vowels (analogous to words like *kata* 'will sing,' but with no consonant between the emic vowels). And the tones contrast: káa 'is climbing', kàa 'metal', káta 'is singing'—the acute as high tone, grave as low, and zero marking as mid tone (compare Pike 1948:79/n).

Etics and emics, that is to say, must enter the analysis of every language at every level of its phonological hierarchy (as well as its grammatical and referential ones). This fact poses a major theoretical and practical challenge to all researchers in language analysis. The answer to the simple question *What is a syllable?* is still difficult—after decades of discussion here and there. How many syllables are in *C'mere!* (*Come here!*)? Or in *'Kyu* (*Thank you*, in some British speech)? Or in *'S cool today!* (*It's cool today!*—compare *school today*)?

To experience this kind of problem for oneself, one may ask a native speaker of Japanese how many syllables, thinking as a Japanese, he hears in the English word *skates*. They have sometimes told me five—seldom fewer than three. They may, in the first case, break it up into something like *sa-ke-ee-ta-sa*; that is, the consonant cluster *sk* may appear to them as a broken down syllable, with a voiceless vowel inserted after the *s-* and before the *-k-*. Few other simple experiments are so accessible to the phonetic layman, and as directly convincing of the need for a *systematic* analysis of language, in place of the normal lay assumption that one merely goes to it to find its sounds.

In Chinatec, referred to earlier in figure 4.3, there can be two kinds of syllables, one with a sharp, quick, let-go decrescendo, and one with a held controlled length; compare (in the pronunciation of some of us) the sharp, short pronunciation of the final syllable of English *celery* or *effigy* versus the long final syllable (perhaps with some kind of secondary or tertiary stress) of *chickadee* (a bird, one morpheme), or *refugee* (grammatically complex—*refuge* plus suffix). There continue to be difficulties in the analysis of syllables, even in English. In some dialects a word like *more* or *mower* or *fear* appears more like two syllables than it does in other dialects of English. Such difficulties, however, should not lead to the discarding of the concept of syllable—which we need very much—but rather to further attention on etic-emic relations, and to the wave character of syllables which allows for *indeterminacies* in segmentation at the borders.

In stress groups, likewise, we can have surprises as we study our own or other languages. In English, in an angry, protesting *That isn't what I said!*, the syllable may be very short and loud, with the *-n't* short and weaker, with much lower pitch; but in a pleading pronunciation of the same sentence, one may hear the opposite—a long, drawn-out *is-*, with a slow drop throughout the rest of the sentence. The Culina language of Peru has a special emphasis type used sometimes under surprise, reflecting a dangerous situation—as in spying a tiger near one (see Pike 1957); the final syllable of the sentence has a sharp, quick rise followed by a sharp, quick fall and decrescendo. In Aguaruna of Peru (Pike 1957) a further pattern comes in the chanting of a shaman. The end of, say, each sentence ends in a quaver (a chanting lilt of voice pitch up and down on the syllable).

## 10.7. Field Characteristics of Phonology Seen via Intonation

We have seen that to view sounds only as isolated chunks is not adequate; they must be sometimes seen as waves overlapping and smearing into each other (figs. 4.1–3), and they must be seen as units in a contrastive system or field (figs. 5.2–4), so that features of tone can be seen as contrasts (fig. 6.4) which lead to choices which can be compared to a person choosing to go through one of several gates (fig. 6.2). In this section we wish to illustrate that even in English a pitch choice is possible also, with a similar set of four gates, or *relative levels of intonation* contrast, but contributing to structures not at the level of syllable nucleus (illustrated for Mazatec in fig. 6.4), but at the level of the stress group. They act not as parts of lexical units such as words or morphemes, but rather as contributing to pitch contours spreading over words, phrases, clauses, or higher units, and contributing to the signaling of *speaker attitude* (or attitude which he attempts to elicit from the hearer).

In general, a rising pitch contour ending an English phrase implies to the hearer that the speaker has not given finality to what he is saying; either he is going to add another phrase (as before a comma), or he is hoping that the hearer will reply (to a question of certain types), or he may be pausing before going further. (Note that I did not say that this is the *only* way these things can be signaled, or that these items *always* signal them; an intersection of various items can cause these normal expectancies to be overridden, in ways beyond the scope of this brief section. For fuller discussion, see Pike 1945.) If, on the other hand, the speaker makes the pitch fall after he has stressed a syllable, he may be calling attention to the importance of the word or phrase which is stressed. If, further, the stressed syllable is followed by unstressed syllables on that same level, there is often an implication that important things are to come or have been left unsaid (either of lovely expectancies or of impending doom). For example, if I say, slowly, *His brain is addled,* with a rise on *brain,* the hearer waits to see what I have to say about that brain. If, rather, I say *His bráin is addled,* with pitch dropping immediately on *brain,* I am singling out the brain rather than some other part (that is, I could add *but his muscles surprisingly enough continue coordinating so that he could still win at the Olympics*). If, on the contrary, I were to say with a completely level mid pitch *Be careful of that boy's brain,* I might be implying *lest you damage it permanently in letting him do that run on the bobsled without wearing a helmet.*

See figure 10.2 (from Pike 1964*b* : 108), where contours at the lower left of the diagonal are all falling, while those on the diagonal itself are level and those to the upper right are rising. That is, each of these major subdivisions has numerous further varieties—with, for example, those including an extra-high pitch involving emphasis or surprise or politeness in some way (for detail and illustrations, see Pike 1945.) The chart as a whole shows a set of English intonation contours as comprising a field structure involving stress and pitch. In that figure we have used *E* for extra-high, *H* for high, *M* for mid, and *L* for low, with a degree sign for the stressed syllable followed by a gradual stepping or gliding down or up (or, in off-norm circumstances of special intensity, with a rapid change).

But these are just a part of the possibilities open to us. We can also have a change point in the middle of a contour, such that we first drop from high to low, and then, without any further stressed syllable intervening, rise (for example, in a contour °H-M-L, as in [*as for the*] *gróove,* where the fall on *groove* singles it out for sharp attention, and the rise on the end of that same syllable leaves the hearer knowing that something is to follow). In addition, there can be unstressed syllables preceding the stressed one, without pause, which help set the stage for the word which has been put into focus by the stress. These pitches carry meanings also, but less strikingly so, and are not shown in figure 10.2 (but see Pike 1945 for discussion of them).

Poets, I feel, should be allowed to say what they think and feel. It should be clear, here, that many scholars do not agree. Part of the meaning of what a man says—often the most important part—is in the intonation. Com-

|     | -E    | -H    | -M    | -L    |
|-----|-------|-------|-------|-------|
| °E- | °E-E  | °E-H  | °E-M  | °E-L  |
| °H- | °H-E  | °H-H  | °H-M  | °H-L  |
| °M- | °M-E  | °M-H  | °M-M  | °M-L  |
| °L- | °L-E  | °L-H  | °L-M  | °L-L  |

*Figure 10.2. Field structure composed of English contours of stressed syllables followed by unstressed ones, in various pitch patterns. The degree sign indicates a stressed syllable; E is extra-high, H is high, M is mid, L is low. To the upper right are rising contours, expressing incompleteness. To the lower left are falling contours, focusing attention on the stressed word or phrase. On the diagonal are level ones, indicating strong implication of something important left unsaid as of that moment (from Pike 1964:108).*

pare, for example, the phrase *That brain of his is magnificent,* spoken with extra-high pitch on the stressed syllable of *magnificent,* then stepping down to low somewhat slowly (impressively), and with appropriate voice quality; it may imply admiration. But the same sentence spoken with the stressed syllable on mid pitch, stepping down to low at the end of the word, and with a snarling voice quality, may imply that the speaker does not believe it and that the man referred to is somewhat of an idiot. Surely such differences are important to a poet. And here we argue that, since many of these meanings are carried by intonation, the right of the poet to express the feelings of his mind carries with it the right to mark his poems for pitch and voice quality—and the added obligation on teachers of English and drama to instruct their students in the mechanisms of utilizing these factors in the writing of poetry, or in writing contrastive ways of speaking a particular bit of a play on stage. Yet when I have suggested this to some teachers, they have resisted the idea, preferring to leave the interpretation rights to the reader and denying them to the poet (whose brain is often assumed to be incapable of this kind of creativity—which in fact may be true of some of this generation and may continue thus until students are taught to be literate in intonation, by being given an intonation alphabet, along with training in its use).

I have tried writing a number of poems marked for pitch in this way (see for example Pike 1967a:61,70) and have made their oral reading available through educational videocassettes (Pike 1977). In figures 10.3–4, however, I give a poem of Emily Dickinson's marked in ways to indicate how it

The 'br|ain within its 'groo·ve

Runs 'evenly and 'true·;/

But |'let a |'splin|ter· 'swerve·.

'Twere |'easier· for 'you·

To 'put· the 'water· 'back·

When 'flood·s have 'slit the 'hills,

And 'scooped a 'turnpike for them 'se·lv·es,

And 'blotted 'out· the 'mi·ll·s!/

*Figure 10.3. Poems may be marked for pitch, as I have done for this one by Emily Dickinson. High pitch is represented by a line just above the letter, mid pitch just below, and low pitch substantially below the letter. A single slash line (as after* true*) suggests that the pitch stays level and steady, rather than falling and fading away. Stress is shown by a vertical stroke before the accented syllable. A raised dot indicates extra length. This reading was by a poet (James Squires) who read it for me very gently and slowly.*

was read for me in quite different ways by James Squires, a poet, and by Austin Warren, a literary critic (for these and a third marking, see Pike 1967*a*:529–30). The reading by the poet was done very quietly with relatively little variation in pitch, and with breaks between the high-level phonological units shown by vowel lengthening (indicated by a raised dot after a consonant or vowel). The reading by the literary critic was much more dramatic, with more pauses, since he felt—he told me—that *every word* is important.

But, as we have implied, voice quality, not just pitch as such, enters into the meaning of the whole. To see how this is suggested crudely, see figure 10.5, where I indicate to the left of one of my own poems a suggestion as to the style of reading of that line.

In order to understand the signals which a speaker sends to a listener, then, the hearer must, in fact, react tacitly to a vast total field structure, largely unknown to him, of intersecting dimensions of acoustic patterns reflecting the movement of the articulatory organs in the formation not only of consonants and vowels but also of pitch, voice quality, rhythm, and pause in relation to hierarchical levels.

At any one point, at any one level, for any one system, some of these matters can be captured in a notation of phonological unit-in-context—the
phonological tagmeme—applied to pronunciation. We close this chapter
by noting, in figure 10.6, just one illustration of this type (from Pike and
Pike 1977:364), where in a poem the slot under focus of the analysis might
be the end of a line, where rhyme ties that line to others.

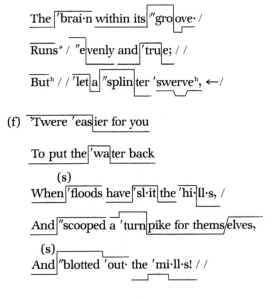

*Figure 10.4. A poem can be read with heightened pitch contrasts, as in
this reading by a literary critic (Austin Warren), one of whose specialities
was the study of Dickinson. The line levels again indicate general pitch
contrasts (not vibrations per second, nor a fixed ratio between them); the
lines between a stressed syllable and an end point or change point are
written as level, for convenience, but in fact may drift gradually up or
down toward the change point. The raised /e/ indicates an added vowel
sound, lightly given, of somewhat the quality of cup; the /ʰ/ is audible
breathiness (when indrawn, an arrow points to the left); the double
slash line is a pause which gives a signal of something being finished
(even though, after true, the sentence is not grammatically finished); the
pitch drifts downward, and the intensity fades. An extra-high pitch is
needed for this reading, shown by an extra-high line. The f means "fast";
the s means "slow."*

| Voice Quality | The Poem Itself: |
|---|---|
| Chanting style: | "The Power is MINE!" |
| Detached, low pitch: | The tyrant chants. |
| With breathiness: | Yet he pants; |
| With short pause groups, and in-drawn breath after each: | Breath/ comes/ short. |
| Tense vocal cords, with lengthened second word: | God squeezes. |
| And pretended sneeze or two during the pronunciation: | Sovereign sneezes . . . |
| With nonverbal breathy exclamation, rising to a crescendo: | And poOf!!! |

*Figure 10.5. Voice quality affects the meaning of a poem. Here in this poem of Pike's (1967c:76) the tension of the vocal cords, breathiness, direction of audible breath intake, crescendo, speed change, and pauses are added to pitch (not shown) for suggesting the effect desired by its author.*

| Slot | Class |
|---|---|
| End of a poetic line, in a rhyming poem | Words ending in a certain set of -VC syllables |
| **Role** | **Cohesion** |
| With the function (in elegant poetry) of calling attention to semantic relations which might not otherwise come to attention | Controlling some agreements of form. For example, in Dickinson, *(h)ills* with *(m)ills*, and *(tr)ue* with *(y)ou* |

*Figure 10.6. A phonological unit-in-context is a tagmeme where pronunciation is involved. The four features (already treated extensively for grammar) show up here on the level of the line-as-a-unit, in a set of lines and words tied by rhyme.*

# 11

# The Referential Hierarchy

We have already mentioned, either directly in relation to the referential hierarchy, or indirectly in relation to meanings or behavior activities which relate to that hierarchy, a number of items: In figure 2.4 the meaning of *jump* is shown as related to the social and physical background. In figure 4.4 the Christmas dinner scene is shown as a continuing wave nucleus over time—which, here, we would treat as a referential constant. The specific identity of Joey as long-nosed, is referential (fig. 6.1), as is the identity of the "same" river in spite of molecular replacements (sec. 7.1), and the girl with changed hairdo (fig. 7.1). So too is the contrastive feature array of semantics for *king* and *queen* (fig. 6.6), or *big sister* (fig. 6.7). These feature arrays are a kind of representation of a field structure within the referential relations, as the Christmas dinner represented a perceived referential wave structure, and as the identity of Joey or of the river captures a component of referential structure in relation to a particle view.

## 11.1. Levels in the Referential Hierarchy

In the grammatical hierarchy we made a sharp break between a proposition of some kind (in the form of clause or sentence) and the mention of a word (for example, a noun labeling a thing, or person, or item); the proposition was considered relatively more independent, and the term relatively more dependent (see secs. 9.2–3). In the phonological hierarchy there was more independence attributed to the syllable than to the phoneme, in an analogous way (sec. 10.2). Now, for the referential hierarchy, we treat as more independent the telling about an *event* than the mention of a *name* of something. Thus the named person *Socrates* is treated on a lower hierarchical level than the *action affirmed* in the sentence *Socrates drank himself to death*; the event as described is treated as higher in rank than the items involved in the event and mentioned in connection with it.

At the lower of these two levels one has, then, the members of the *cast* of a play or of an event. And these members are—in the normal, basic situation—*particular* members mentioned in a particular play or a particular event. The particular members of the cast may be—if well enough known—entered into an *encyclopedia*. There one could find various Henrys of history—each of them a different person; or various Johns—for example, as different popes. Each would be a different referential entity, although the *name* would be the same *lexically,* and hence identical in each occurrence in so far as its membership in a grammatical class (personal noun) is concerned.

But there is a further, crucial difference between grammatical and referential units at this point. The lexical item *Socrates* must remain as a noun, the same noun, in all its occurrences. But as simultaneously representing—for the moment—a referential item, it has great flexibility of *paraphrase* without loss of its referential identity, even though it is no longer a noun. Thus one can say *You know, the man I was talking to you about that Plato wrote about,* or *I refer to Plato's teacher who had to drink the hemlock,* or even *You know who I mean,* or *the great Socrates,* or *he.* Notice, however, that these are accepted by the hearer (or reader) *only if the specific context warrants it* and allows the participants (speaker and hearer) in the discussion to be satisfied that the same person is being talked about. It is *their* (emic) judgment of the identity, not that of someone who is an outsider to the conversation, which provides the appropriate criteria for the referential identification involved.

Note further that the fact that a unit of the referential hierarchy can be paraphrased in numerous different grammatical forms is crucial evidence that referential and grammatical hierarchies are *not the same,* since they often are *nonisomorphic* (for phonology versus grammar, see fig 10.1). Their forms are often different (even though necessarily homophonous in some of their manifestations), since *every* manifestation (mention) of a referential unit *must* be in *some* grammatical form; the difference is that the emically same referential item may be in many *different* grammatical forms.

On the other hand, there is a parallel: As grammar can have the paired levels of word and phrase, both of which are terms, so the referential level of identity (Jones 1977) can have a particular member of a cast belonging to a larger group in the cast: Socrates was a member of a philosophical group, and as a child he belonged to some kind of biological and social family group with father and mother. At the higher level too there are parallels. As the grammatical level of proposition can have a clause (which if independent and unmodified can be simultaneously a particular kind of simple sentence, by disjunct definition) paired with complex sentences of various types, so an event may be part of a larger event, which in turn is part of a still larger event. In addition, a more complex situation frequently is relevant on the higher level: Two "separate" events may be occurring at the same time, which later turn out to merge into a single event. (*Boy* [with one history] *meets girl* [with a different history]; *they fall in love, marry, and live happily ever after.*) Such a *merging event complex* also serves as a unit of the referential hierarchy analogous to the complex sentence (or even higher unit) of grammar.

Background expectancies can be forced to merge in the hearer's mind by the speaker's use of a pun. Thus *Socrates drank himself to death* merges the expectancies raised by the mention of the dialogues of Plato with the expectancies caused by the mention of excessive use of liquor. They can also merge, on a much more serious level, when an author acts as a member of a cast in the performance of a play which he has himself written—a kind of literary incarnation in his own creation. (For an elegant referential analysis of a Carib, Guatemala, folktale in which a related situation is analyzed, along with extensive hierarchical treatment of the housing arrangement, social involvement, and tagmeme formulas of a referential type, see Howland 1981.)

For a lower level of the referential hierarchy than that of the identity (or person or prop or item), I tried using *contrastive features* of a unit (that is, elements of its physical or semantic *componential analysis*) as seen by the analyst or as seen and commented on by a native actor serving as a lay analyst of some item on his own culture. There is no break in the theory from the discussion of the philosopher or linguist to the discussion of the man in the street or the preliterate speaker of a language. (See figs. 5.2−6 and 6.6−7 for charts whose rows and columns are labeled for features of phonology, of grammar, of semantics, or of poetry. An extensive summary of the bibliography of semantic features is found in Nida 1975.) That is, once an item is abstracted from the normal contexts of its being used and is focused on by an analyst for discovering or describing its inner properties, the *named concept*, in its various paraphrases, thus abstracted becomes an element of the referential hierarchy at the level of identity (cast, person, item), whereas *its* contrastive features in turn become elements of a level below that one. Recently, however, Evelyn Pike has felt that we should treat contrastive features as components of units at *every* level of *each* hierarchy. Then, for the level below that of identities in the *referential* hierarchy, we might place *relationships*. This might include, among others, the relationship between an attribute and an entity, or a geographical relation between two entities, or the direction of action of an entity toward or from a place or thing.

## 11.2. The Referential Tagmeme

Just as slot, class, role, and cohesion were useful in the analysis of grammar (fig. 9.3) and of phonology (fig. 10.6), so the scheme is useful here. *Purpose,* for example, finds its place in the role cell, in the description of an event; and so likewise does the relevance in the description of a member of the cast or of a prop. On the event level it is relevant, for example, that a joke is *intended* when one says *Socrates drank himself to death.* On the level of cast, likewise, it is relevant to know who is the hero—or the villain—in a film (and unless one does know, one cannot understand the outcome of many stories or films). That is, the role cell may be filled explicitly by the analyst, or tacitly by the naive reader; pure formal analysis without reference to meaning or purpose or relevance cannot provide an analysis which can satisfy those who wish to know sensibly "what happened."

Such roles can be complicated. An event may have a purpose leading to a larger purpose; or motives may be mixed (dual). And a person's role may appear different from the point of view of different observers, each of whom has his own *interpretations* of (or guesses about) the purposes of others. Thus, in the referential realm, we may sometimes discuss the actions of different observers separately, since their purposes are different (see, for several different *levels* of observer, Pike 1981).

An event as described may enter a marginal slot in a series of events leading toward the crucial, nuclear event under attention. The item filling that slot of the description is one member of the paraphrase set identifiable by the speaker as (emically) the same from his point of view, and as acceptable as a replacement for it in this place in his account, or in other places of that same account (see Fig. 11.1).

But for the narration of an event to be intelligible to a hearer, there must be a degree of cohesion of *actual expectancies* of the hearer with the expectancies expected *of* him by the speaker, and a degree of coherence—if the hearer thinks that facts are being recounted—with the view of reality as believed in by the hearer. If the speaker is perceived by the hearer as having no such coherence (and no joking intent, for example), the hearer may

WHERE the subevent occurred, as nuclear or marginal to the including event: here, nuclear, as a subevent of the larger event of *The meeting at the prison* (69):

> in the prison with Socrates on the day when he drank the poison [67]

the crowning point at the end of a dialogue which included a discussion of the possibility of avoiding it.

WHAT happened, emically defined as being members of a paraphrase set acceptable to the narrator:

> when he drank the poison [67];
> Then raising the cup to his lips, quite readily and cheerfully he drank of the poison [159].

---

WHY the actor performed the event—or the cause deduced by the narrator:

> I have spoken many words in the endeavor to show you that when I have drunk the poison I shall leave you and go to the joys of the blessed. [156]

In this discussion, furthermore, his purpose was to put truth above life and above his own reputation; and his wish was to push others to truth:

> And I would ask you [he said] to be thinking of the truth and not of Socrates; agree with me, if I seem to you to be speaking the truth; or if not, withstand me might and main, that I may not deceive you as well as myself in my enthusiasm, and like the bee, leave my sting in you before I die. [120]

HOW the event coheres with the underlying belief system of the narrator, or of the hearer as expected or reported of him by the narrator (or with truth as seen by the "outside" analyst in relation to some other frame of reference):

> Why should he [the real philosopher] repine at that which he had been always pursuing and desiring [i.e., death and dying] [76], with death in which the soul is released from the body and the body is released from the soul. [77]

*Figure 11.1. A referential event tagmeme in which the subevent occurs as merely one tagmeme in a series which represents the larger event: the dialogue of friends with Socrates, when in the jail they tried to persuade him not to drink the hemlock. The larger particular-event setting gives the slot. The larger background setting gives cohesion to—and in part controls—the whole, and makes sense out of it. The specific purpose of the specific actor under attention (Socrates) provides the data for the role cell. A set of paraphrases are taken from Jowett's translation of the Dialogues of Plato, or from the introduction to it by Kaplan (1952); page numbers refer to that edition.*

| WHERE the member of the cast fits a larger unit of the cast: | WHAT the cast member is named, as a member of a paraphase set appropriate to this narrative: |
|---|---|
| Socrates as the nuclear member of the discussion group, in the prison, along with Phaedo, Apollodorus, Simmias, Cebes, Crito, and an attendant. | Socrates, a friend, he, him, his, I, me, my, you, yourself; [Kaplan:] ethical leader of the young and unflagging conscience of the rulers and citizens of Athens [ix], the main figure in most of the dialogues [xi], the seventy-year-old Socrates. [2] |
| THE FUNCTION OR ROLE of the cast member as he sees himself, or is seen by others, or by the narrator: | HOW the cast member is related to an underlying belief system which affects his actions: |
| of all men of his time whom I have known, he was the wisest and justest and best. [160] | therefore let the cup be brought . . . for I do not think that I should gain anything by drinking the poison a little later; I should only be ridiculous in my own eyes for sparing and saving a life which is already forfeit' [158]; 'I ought to be grieved at death, if I were not persuaded in the first place that I am going to other gods who are wise and good . . . I do not grieve . . . for I have good hope that there is yet something remaining for the dead, and as has been said of old, some far better thing for the good than for the evil. [75] |

*Figure 11.2. A referential person tagmeme, the principal speaker in the dialogues of Plato; characterized in the* Phaedo *as the nuclear member of a small discussion group in the prison at the time of the death scene, with the role of a wise man who has a belief about afterlife which affects and controls his sayings at the time of his drinking the poison. The paraphase set which includes* Socrates *includes also the pronouns used by himself and others, as well as indirect reference to him as a friend and the characterizations of him in notes by Kaplan. Other tagmemic characterizations could have been made of the prison itself, the poison, and the setting as a whole. (Page numbers refer to Kaplan 1952.)*

judge the speaker to be insane or lying. Here, then, *truth* and falsehood, relative to a given *frame of reference,* find their way into the description.

Each referential level will have its own tagmemes. Like an event, so also a member of the cast may be represented in relation to slot, class, role, and cohesion (see fig. 11.2 for Socrates treated this way, in relation to the dialogue *Phaedo*).

## 11.3. Some Grammatical and Phonological Alternatives in the Representation of Referential Talking Space

We assume here that a person lives in *referential space*—in interlocking tacit or implicit frames of reference of *time* sequence, *spatial* array, *physical* relationships, *logical* coherence, *social* structures, *psychological* involvement, *belief* systems about reality, *intersecting events,* and others. No person can bring into words all at one moment the content of each of these in all its detail. Selection must be made if one is to talk at all; the balance must be left unstated at that moment, even though it remains as a strong force controlling much of the talk.

Furthermore, within any one language or culture the *ordering* of the talking presentation of any one of these frame types will be considered here the *normal* (or basic) order when it is the first learned in childhood or most frequently used later. But off-norm forms of presentation may occur when the speaker has some reason (tacit or explicit) for selecting a less basic item for highlighting, since at that moment, to him, it seems important beyond its normal place in the hierarchical or sequential or matrix structure of the frame as a whole. When this happens, the special focus desired can be obtained by special grammatical arrangements, or they may be forced, in part, by the place of the item in the larger discourse or by the emotional reaction of the speaker.

In a classical syllogism, for example, major and minor premises are followed by a conclusion: *All men are mortal; Socrates was a man; therefore, Socrates was mortal.* A belief system underlies the premises of such a syllogism. If this belief seems to someone to be challenged, and if he is outraged by it, the syllogism may be reordered, as in the following interaction between two speakers:

*First speaker:*    Socrates lives on!
*Second speaker:*  Socrates? He died! He was a man, wasn't he? (And don't all men die?)

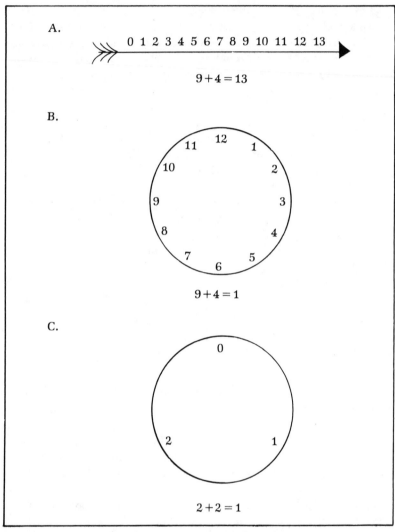

*Figure 11.3. The truth of a statement is not to be confused with the cor-rectness of its grammatical form; it must rather be judged relative to the frame of reference within which it is stated. Here, the addition of 9 + 4 in relation to the model of a line gives 13 (A); on a clock face of 12 hours, it gives 1 (1:00) (B); on a clock face with 0 and 2 hours, 2 + 2 gives 1 (C). (Metaphor, likewise, may carry truth judged relative to the joint expec-tancies of speaker-hearer acting within the same frame of reference of expectancies, intent, and literary genre.)*

The grammatical structure is radically altered in the utterance of the second speaker by the order of its elements (with conclusion first), by the change from statement to question, by the optional occurrence of the first premise (as shown by the parentheses), by the change of focus (with attention to the man and to the fact of his death), by the emotional overtones (of expostulation), and by the deliberate or pretended misunderstanding of the first by the second speaker (where the second takes the first literally rather than figuratively).

The underlying syllogism is unchanged; but the change of speaker-to-audience relations, implicit in the second telling, is a referential change superimposed upon the syllogism itself. (Here we have referential levels of observer relevance; see Pike 1981). Here, as in many other instances, a change in pronunciation (for example, the exclamatory form) may help alert the listener to know that an off-norm form of grammar or of reference or of their interrelation is occurring.

## 11.4. Reality Relative to a Frame of Reference, versus Grammatical Form

It is important not to confuse correctness of formation of a sentence grammatically with truth relative to a particular referential framework. A statement can be factually correct, or true, even though badly stated. And a lie can be elegantly framed by a con man to cheat a victim. In terms of the theory presented here, it is grammatically correct to say *Plato drank the poison*—fully as correct grammatically as to say *Socrates drank the poison*—but false to our referential belief about history. The primary student, then, must not be accused of bad grammar when his word arrangements are impeccable but his sums are faulty (see fig. 11.3, where nine plus four equals thirteen or one, relative to a particular frame of reference).

It is important, therefore, in listening, to seek to understand the intent and general frame of discourse of the author. Jones (1977:v), for example, discusses theme in expository discourse "in terms of nuclearity in the referential hierarchy"; and she treats theme as "referential prominence" but focus as "grammatical prominence" (pp. vi–vii). She also deals with "grammatical devices for highlighting theme" (pp. 169–223).

Understanding may disappear for listeners when respective frames of understanding of the universe differ for speaker and listener, but it can be the source of shared humor when both speaker and listener know that deliberate incongruity of frames of reference is involved (see fig. 11.4).

A. The moon is more important than the sun—the moon gives light by night when it's needed—the sun during the day when it's light anyhow.

B. *A drunk, running around a tree three times:* I'm lost in the impenetrable forest.

C. *Psychiatrist:* Tell me sir, why are you standing on one foot?
*Patient:* If I lifted the other one I'd fall down.

D. *A man, to the barber, when he had been nicked by the razor:* Give me a glass of water, please.
*Barber:* Why?
*Man:* I want to see if my neck leaks.

*Figure 11.4. Unless the frame of reference is shared and coherent, there may be misunderstanding, error, or humor. In A there is implied lack of knowledge on the part of the purported speaker, understood by the listener as being humorous error. In B the misunderstanding of the physical situation by the speaker is attributed by the hearer to the influence of liquor on the speaker. In C the speaker is assumed to be out of touch with reality for mental reasons. In D we are supposed to imagine the barber listening to the wry humor directed at him, involving a deliberate—and caustic—implication of known (shared) implicit impossibility. In E there is further subtlety—the listener pretends to understand, pretends to reinforce sympathetically the speaker's claim, but in fact jabs back with an implicit vicious attack.*

# IV

## Context

# Introduction to Part IV

A field view of a discipline as an intersection of various parameters of analyst viewpoint on the world outside of him has the great advantage of flexibility. One can come at the data from various theoretical or empirical directions, and therefore mine a richness and multiple interlocking cohesion of principles which is lacking if one attempts to follow a single rigid logical sequence of presentation (or a single presumed real taxonomy or rule structure of objective reality) apart from observer choice (or the arbitrariness of temporary analyst-observer interests changing according to the needs of the moment or of the era). On the other hand, for a person who wants a tightly organized nonoverlapping approach such a view is disconcerting. Nothing in it seems stable, everything seems everything else, and observer freedom seems to be the death of scientific detachment and precision. Even the fact that over the eras the views of scientific truth change radically (and the certainty of then-certain facts) does not deter him from obtaining intellectual peace by a commitment to a scientific truth which will not last—but which for the moment is popular (or, stated more elegantly, is the current dominant paradigm—compare Kuhn 1962).

One can avoid many problems of the moment and pacify the snarls of a dominant scientific paradigm by agreeing to accept its overpowering postulates. ("Do you want to know a sure way to conciliate a tiger? Let him swallow you.") But if those postulates cancel the possibility of including the observer himself in the situation and among the data observed, and hence of observer flexibility in choice of viewpoint and in the possibility of adopting different viewpoints for different purposes of the moment, one has allowed his scientific freedom to be swallowed up and science itself to become *nothing but* an unattainable abstract ideal in a dreamed-of unreachable reductionism, or else in an abstracting idealism which splits me from you, us from things, and things from human knowledge.

The next three chapters cover some of the same data as seen earlier. This is inevitable, in tagmemic theory, since *each* of its perspectives covers *all* the same data—as we began to show in the chapters on particle, wave, and field. Here, then, I add emphases rather than new material. In Chapter 12 there is emphasized the necessity of keeping form and meaning together—in contrast with some other schools of thought. In Chapter 13 I discuss change again, but with emphasis on the fact that change does not occur in the absence of a framework (or of bumping, or merging, or sharing, or some other way of bridging the gap between the items involved). In Chapter 14, higher-level frames are under attention—the universes of discourse within which rational talk can occur.

# 12

## Form-and-Meaning

In this chapter I am rejecting all views of language or life which claim that *abstract* forms comprise basic reality. Here, as over against centuries of work by some scholars, *form* is a term used to refer to concretely structured elements which include a physical component, not idealized disembodied realities, essences, ideas—or even rules or relations. In addition to form, a meaning, relevance, value, significance, deduced cause, result of deduced cause, or some other *observer-related component* is always demanded in our affirmation of the existence of any unit of rational behavior, of the existence of the observability of any concrete object or event, or of any object or event as deduced by man or imagined by man.

### 12.1 Meaning as Essentially Tied to a Physical Component in a Unit

Each unit (see Part II) of each level of each hierarchy—grammatical, phonological, and referential—has a physical component. In tagmemic theory there is no semantic hierarchy abstracted away from all physical manifestation; the referential hierarchy is not a semantic one *per se,* but is a different and *simultaneous* structuring of the *same stuff,* which is also structured by the grammatical and phonological hierarchies (see also the combination of form and meaning as discussed in sec. 2.5). Suppose, for example, that we read aloud onto tape the sentence *Socrates died after he'd drunk the poison.* If we were to scissor and snip away each sound (or syllable or stress group) one after another, what would be left? Nothing. If we take a second copy of the tape and snip away the grammatical dependent and independent clauses (or the conjunctions, subjects, predicates, and objects), what would be left? Nothing. If, from a third copy, we snip away the stated causing subevent (the drinking of the poison, which happened—but was not stated—first), then the stated effect subevent (the dying, which happened second but which was stated first), what would be left? Nothing. There are, then, in this view three separate structurings of the same substance, but structurings which may or may not have the same beginnings and endings or sequential (or other) relationships of all or of some of their parts (for nonisomorphic grammar and phonology, see also fig. 10.1).

## 12.2. Hierarchically Extended Lexicon as the Substance Manifesting, Simultaneously, the Forms of the Three Hierarchies

The substance shared by grammar, phonology, and reference we call *lexicon*. But the term carries more meaning, in this context, than that of mere dictionary listing; rather, it includes the *particular utterance or part of an utterance under attention* at the moment, provided that it is a unit containing at least one morpheme. It may be a single morpheme, as *had*, or a variant (allomorph) of that morpheme, as *'d*; or a phrase such as *had drunk*; or an entire particular sentence (*not* the abstract pattern of a sentence); or an entire poem or discourse in its particularity. That is, by hierarchical extension of the lexicon we mean the *particular* language-manifested elements at any level of the hierarchy, whether dictionary entries (*lexicon proper*), or phrases, sentences, discourses, or conversations.

Meanings in language as used by the man in the street are treated as features relevant to behavioral impact, including the elicitation of understanding. In grammar, these may include the meanings of role (function) of a tagmeme (as in secs. 9.4–5, figs. 9.3–4). In phonology, it can come from the impact of voice quality (see fig. 10.5). In reference, it includes the meaning of lexicon (fig. 2.4), contrastive features of lexicon (figs. 6.6–7), or meanings of particular words, phrases, sentences, poems, discourses, or conversations. Each of the units manifesting each level of each hierarchy carries some kind of behavioral impact. Here, each of these is treated as a meaning of some kind, as part of a concrete unit manifesting the form of one of the hierarchies.

In figure 12.1 I try to suggest this relationship (building on suggestions

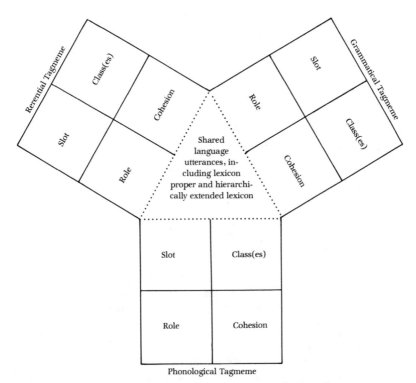

Phonological Tagmeme

*Figure 12.1. Hierarchies of reference, grammar, and phonology are not abstracted from shared substance, but retain the physical component contributed by the particular speech event itself. An emic utterance is a behaviorally meaningful simultaneous combination of three structures which share their momentary lexical manifestation including lexicon, extended hierarchically to embrace the reading of a poem or the presentation of a lecture.*

from Evelyn Pike—see Pike and Pike 1977:365) by a triangle labeled as this lexical shared substance of language utterances, but with tagmemic four-celled rectangles sprouting from each of the sides, representing the respective hierarchies. The dots on the triangle sides suggest that the lexical item is *part of* all three of the hierarchies at the same time. It is a concrete form-meaning behavioral composite we are dealing with, not a set of abstractions away from substance. (A comparable point could be made by using the figure of a cube; its three dimensions would represent the three hierarchies, intersecting in specific utterances, which represent the three dimensions simultaneously.)

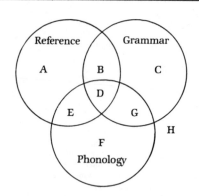

A. *Mary:* I didn't say yes to John the first time he proposed.
   *Susan:* Yes, I know—you weren't there, my dear.
B. *(Mother puts diaper on baby, without powder) Child:* Mommy, you forgot to salt him.
C. What is it that the more it dries the wetter it gets? A towel.
D. Why is the electric chair period furniture? Because it ends a sentence.
E. Why do Swiss cows wear bells? Because their horns don't work.
F. She must be in her middle flirties.
G. What is a cross between an abalone and a crocodile? A crock of bologney.
H. Why are three leaves from a stone? Because an elephant sighs.

*Figure 12.2. Prominence given to the hierarchies differs from one joke to another. Any one of the three may be exploited for the unexpectedness of its relationships; or any combination may be used. In A, no pun—no phonology—is involved, but the implication—not expected by Mary— is that John had earlier proposed to someone else. In B, the child confuses talcum powder with salt, referentially, and expresses this in a referential-grammatical idiom. In C, the term* dries *is grammatically first intransitive, then transitive (that is, it* dries *something). In D, there is a triple pun (period as a unit of time or punctuation, sentence as a grammatical unit or a judge's verdict, ends as in ending a life or a written utterance). In E the attention shifts from pasture needs to the pseudoneeds of warning by blowing horns, by way of the phonology (the pun). In F the phonology mixes flirt with thirties, making up a new lexical item, flirties. In G there is a switch from two words (abalone and crocodile) to a noun with a phrase modifier (a crock of baloney) by way of partial phonetic similarity, fused. In H there is no natural or focused coherence of grammar, phonology, or reference between question and answer, so that the noncoherence is itself intended to be puzzling, and hence "funny." Some people would call this a shaggy dog story.*

## 12.3. Humor via Focus on Intersecting Form and Meaning in Hierarchies

The relationships, however, are much more complex than can be seen in figure 1. If we ignore for the moment the details of the four-celled elements and treat their relation only in relation to the momentary prominence of one or more of the three hierarchies, we can also show this intersection by means of a Venn diagram, as in figure 12.2. Humor is there classified in relation to the kinds of hierarchical sharing which are especially *in focus* for a particular joke. (All three hierarchies are present in each joke, but one or more are selected for special attention.)

> *Query:* Why is getting up at four o'clock in
> the morning like a pig's tail?
> *Answer:* It's [twŕli].

Here, if *twirlly* and *too early* are deliberately pronounced alike, the single phonological answer to both implies two different simultaneous lexicogrammatical-referential answers, referring respectively to the two parts of the question.

## 12.4. Form and Meaning Interlocking in Poetry

Poetry, like humor, exploits the relations between the simultaneous hierarchies. It uses phonology to force to attention (of the composing writer, then the reader) certain normally unexpected connections which may carry pleasure, shock, or depth of understanding. In figure 12.3 I give a poem of mine in which referential connections are suggested by rhyme and in which grammatical form is affected by the pretended discourse structure (that of a telegram, cutting out various minor words). As for grammar, for example, note the lack of a subject before the verb *need* (even though it is not an imperative clause), justified by the telegraphic form; and note lack of subject and verb auxiliary *I am* before *feeling queer*. See also the balance—an essential property of poetry—of *hoping* and *waiting*, as a kind of grammar rhyme. As for phonological elements, there is not only rhyme balancing the second and third lines of both stanzas (*here—queer, quick—sick*) but a tie to the referential implication (that is, implication: *Since you're not here, I feel queer;* and *Unless you come quick, I'll get sick*). Unless the rhyme forces attention to referential meaning to lock words into a universe of discourse and cohesion in some way, rhyming poetry can become mere jingle. (Note, also, that the capital letters help suggest the tele-

**TELEGRAM**

CAN YOU COME
NEED YOU HERE
FEELING QUEER
HOPING.
GRAB A TRAIN
MAKE IT QUICK
I'LL GET SICK
WAITING.

*Figure 12.3. A poem interlocks form and meaning in an intricate complex vastly more variable than can be handled by a fixed set of rules or cross-hierarchical mappings to predict them. The poem is by Pike.*

graphic format.) Referentially, in addition, the first lines of the two stanzas balance, with parallelism of *come* (using a query as a semicommand) with *grab a train* (as direct indication of command to implement the implicit command-request). Similarly, the suggestion of illness (*need you . . . feeling queer*) is more fully developed in the second stanza (*I'll get sick waiting*).

But in poetry as in jokes, in seriousness as in humor, I do not treat an abstract semantic component divorced from the concrete body of expression. Meaning is tied to form, so that it exists only where there is form of some kind; it is never postulated either apart from form or apart from an observer who emically structures the concrete or pretended material which he sees, imagines he sees, deduces the presence of, or creates in nightmare or in science fiction. The interrelationships of grammatical arrangement, phonological manifestation, and referential emically significant event, person, or prop are tied to the presence of an observer as part of the total situation. The linguist is just one observer among others, including the native speaker.

In handling data such as those implied in the appreciation of a small total poem (not just its separate sentences), its concrete, physically manifested words, sentences, rhymes, and background experiences are relevant, along with its meaning, implications, author intent (where known), and reader interpretation (where known). This leads to differences between tagmemic theory, with its emic generalizations and notation, and those theories which offer a quasi-mathematical abstraction of rules or symbolic systems away from such concreteness and observer relevance. The difference is clearly seen, perhaps, by contrasting this preference of mine with a statement by Chomsky (1962:129), in which *symbols only* explicitly comprise his philosophical and procedural focus:

Motivated now by the goal of constructing a grammar, instead of a rule of procedure for constructing an inventory of elements, we no longer have any reason to consider the symbols 'NP', 'sentence', a 'VP', etc., that appear in these rules to be names of certain classes, sequences, or sequences of classes of *concrete* elements. They are *simply* elements in a system of *representation* which has been constructed so as to enable us to characterize effectively the set of English sentences in a linguistically meaningful way. [Italics added]

Compare also Chomsky and Morris Halle, in a preface to Chomsky 1966: "the purely formal aspects of *language, envisaged as a mathematical object*" [italics added].

My own view seems to be more related to an approach by a physicist than to one by a mathematician or logician. *Purely* formal aspects of a poem—or of any other manifestation of language—do not satisfy my interests, excitements, or applied needs, no matter how helpful they have been and continue to be in deepening the understanding of the discipline in many phases of language. I seek, therefore, for a balance of attention between form (including physical and systemic relations and contexts) and meaning (including behavioral impact from the three hierarchies of grammar, phonology, and reference). The four-cell tagmemic notation is a component of our attempt to tackle these concerns.

I would have comparable reactions to any view of language, therefore, which might treat it as exclusively made up of relations of relations of relations (with no given theoretical stopping point) or to a view of language which assumes that one can *first* treat all of meaning, and then and then only appropriately study the relation of that meaning to manifesting form. Tagmemic theory affirms that language contains and is composed of emic form-meaning composites.

# 13

## Sharing as Prerequisite to Change

We live in a universe of physically flowing, merging, smearing, overlapping perceived entities. We live in a universe of waves (Chapter 4). No view which deals *exclusively* with perceived sharp-cut units, things, classes can handle Heraclitus's river (see sec. 7.1), the merging of phonemes (figure 4.2), or the intersection of phonology, grammar, and reference (Chapter 12). Logical partitioning has a necessary place in perception, when the observer "sees" particles (Chapter 3) as if they were completely separate. But it must not be allowed to become the logical tiger which swallows us (Introduction to Part IV).

### 13.1 Change Involving the Sharing of Particles

When two syllables are viewed as a pair of waves in sequence, rapid speech may make them merge at their borders. This can lead to temporary or permanent change in the phonemic content of morphemes manifested by syllables in such a way that a new sound—not present in either, under different or slower conditions—is shared. Thus in the phrase *as you like* (/æz yu lá'k/), both /z/ and /y/ may disappear and be replaced by /ž/ (as in *azure*). The two morphemes, and the two syllables, both share the one newly present sound. Here the meaning is unchanged, and no unexpected shift of attention occurs. Speed-induced fusion such as this, if retained, may lead to a permanent change of morphemic phonological shape.

In a pun, on the other hand, the fact of sharing is a deliberate part of the communication—which by design forces a change from thinking of one imagined or expected situation to thinking of another. Suppose, for example, that we ask:

Catt'll = cattle

'Why is a mouse like a pile of hay?'
'The cat'll eat it.' or 'The cattle eat it.'

Figure 13.1. In a pun, two different sentences can share the same form of pronunciation. Out of context, the utterance manifesting either one is ambiguous with the other. In a pun, the ambiguity is designed to force a change of attention from one area to another (expected to unexpected) or to force a vibration of attention between two possible understandings.

> Question: Why did the widow with two sons name her ranch "Focus"?
> Answer: That's where the sons raise meat.
> Or: That's where the sun's rays meet.

The alternative answers may be pronounced exactly alike. That is, in the reply, the *single utterance* (physical item) could be the manifestation of *either* of *two different sentences* (form-meaning composites); the two share the same phonological particles. (For another illustration, see fig. 13.1.) The genre relies on this fact.

## 13.2. Change Involving the Sharing of Wave Components

From a different perspective, the preceding illustrations can be viewed as the sharing of waves—since a sound can be seen as a wave, as can a syllable. So I turn to a much different kind of wave—a *wave of meaning* of a lexical item, which was mentioned earlier in connection with *run* in section 4.3. There, the lexical meaning of a word was viewed as changeable, with a *central* (normal) meaning, and one or more marginal meanings. Here, however, we are interested in its meaning variants as involving the influence of context.

The *central* meaning will usually be considered the one which is learned earliest in life, is used most frequently, is most physical in its reference, and is used analytically as the most convenient basis for descriptive order or rule derivation. When the criteria clash, different analysts may reach different conclusions—which will in general be mechanically convertible the one to the other, communicable across theories or descriptions, and each useful in its applied context. Such judgments are usually—and usefully—made on the basis of the intuition of the analyst or of the native speaker, subject to changing judgments as more instances are brought to attention. The centrality versus marginality of meaning—the wave character—of *run* can be suggested by figure 13.2. In its marginal usages, the word *run* is found to share (or be modified by) some component of meaning implied in the context containing it; simultaneously, the word may affect the meaning of the contextual words. When an object is added to a clause, *run* may be transformed metaphorically from *(a person himself) running to a place* into *(a person) forcing something which has no feet to move;* the added grammatical transitivity there affects the meaning of the verb, as in *to run*

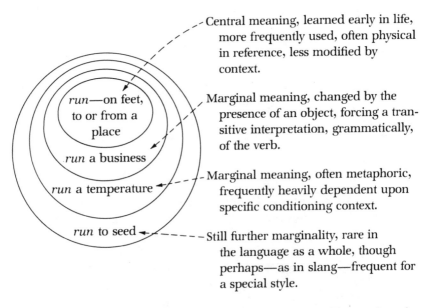

Central meaning, learned early in life, more frequently used, often physical in reference, less modified by context.

Marginal meaning, changed by the presence of an object, forcing a transitive interpretation, grammatically, of the verb.

Marginal meaning, often metaphoric, frequently heavily dependent upon specific conditioning context.

Still further marginality, rare in the language as a whole, though perhaps—as in slang—frequent for a special style.

*Figure 13.2. A change in meaning-viewed-as-wave is forced by its shared context, whether that be physical, mental, social, or linguistic.*

A. Mother's admonition to city child.

B. Child's comment, upon seeing pigs, later, in the country.

*Figure 13.3. The sharing of a referential component of eating style can lead to a metaphor, a socially marginal meaning of a wave of meaning.*

*a business*. The change can go further, to instances where the running and the item changing it are both metaphorical, as in *to run to seed*, where *seed* has little to do with the person affected, but suggests that life's productive period has ended.

The background (physical, mental, social, linguistic) within which a word (or other unit) has been learned may *force* a change from the socially accepted central meaning to a personal marginal one. The choice of native-speaker norm is often dependent upon the history of the speaker's own experience, or solidified into a dead metaphor by the past experience and usage of the community, when accompanied by loss of the original environment stimulus for the old change. In figure 13.3 the context is the city training of the child versus the country training (considered to be the society norm, in this instance); the original marginal meaning has now become the central one for the off-norm child. The word *pig* as meaning an animal has come to mean, for the city child, a sloppily eating child. The city child's experience of hearing the term has been related to contexts in which its eating style has been objected to by the parent. The child then uses its particularized interpretation of norm to interpret the meaning of the word *pig* when it senses the physical characteristics shared by pig and self. (Based on a lost reference somewhere in Bloomfield's work—but remembered because of shared amusement at the shift in sharing.)

## 13.3. Change Involving the Sharing of Field Components

In Chapter 5 we showed field structures in terms of two-dimensional diagrams, with contrastive features as rows and columns for sounds (figs. 5.2–4), grammatical clauses (fig. 5.5), and for a referential poetic structure (fig. 5.6). Later we used comparable charts for showing contrastive semantic features of words (figs. 6.6–7). If one restricts oneself to just one entrance into such a matrix, one can transform the chart into a tree structure. This has the advantage that one particular set of relationships is selected and clearly diagramed and gives the basis for a useful *taxonomy* of *part* embedded in *whole,* with *species* differentiated from *genus.* Such taxonomies are used again and again in scientific work of many kinds. In addition, they can be used to describe the talked-about world of a group of speakers whose native taxonomy is very different from our own. In figure 13.4 a brief suggestion is given of the way such an approach can be used to partition a universe of experience.

A difficulty with such diagrams, however, may appear when certain characteristics are seen to be shared by two branches of the tree *after* they have been separated; if the branches are twigs far separated, the feature may be awkward to describe. The implication is that such a *simple tree approach is inadequate* for representing some of the complexities of behavior as lived. This can lead to surprise at unexpected relations, when expectation has been built on a tree instead of matrix relations, to a disillusioned rejection of an elsewhere useful taxonomy, or to the desirability of supplementary rephrasing of a problem in dimensional matrix terms. In figure 13.5 I give one instance where the expectancy of the *non*occurrence of a characteristic, on the basis of experienced differentiation in the projected taxonomy, is fatal when in fact that characteristic is shared by the two branches.

An n-dimensional matrix gives more flexibility than does a tree diagram for the observer to choose alternative sets of viewing priorities (alternative entrance points or directions into the matrix) at different particular moments, for different needs and interests. Instead of talking about plant versus animal, and cat versus dog or mouse, one may wish to discuss temporarily various divisions of creatures according to hair types, for example.

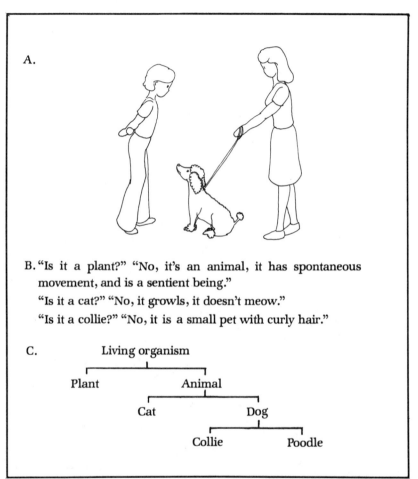

A.

B. "Is it a plant?" "No, it's an animal, it has spontaneous movement, and is a sentient being."
"Is it a cat?" "No, it growls, it doesn't meow."
"Is it a collie?" "No, it is a small pet with curly hair."

C.

*Figure 13.4. A taxonomic tree illustrates one way of partitioning a conceptual universe into genus and species. It has the advantage of leading to clear-cut logical definition, but the disadvantage of imposing (for the moment at least) one viewpoint, one set of priority criteria; and it may conceal implicitly some characteristics—important for other purposes—shared by twigs far removed from each other in the diagram.*

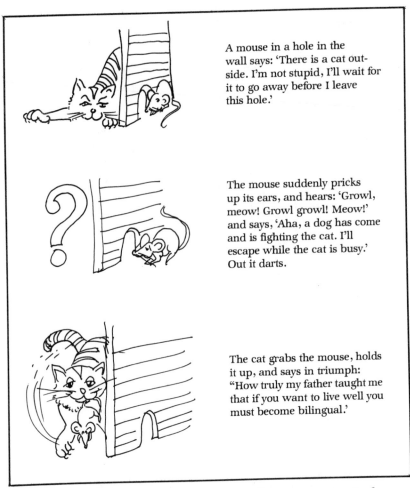

A mouse in a hole in the wall says: 'There is a cat outside. I'm not stupid, I'll wait for it to go away before I leave this hole.'

The mouse suddenly pricks up its ears, and hears: 'Growl, meow! Growl growl! Meow!' and says, 'Aha, a dog has come and is fighting the cat. I'll escape while the cat is busy.' Out it darts.

The cat grabs the mouse, holds it up, and says in triumph: "How truly my father taught me that if you want to live well you must become bilingual.'

*Figure 13.5. The cat's sharing of a taxonomic feature—a capacity for growling which is normally attributed only to dogs—catches the mouse by surprise. In trusting to his taxonomy, here too simple, the mouse loses his life to the "bilingual" cat.*

The mind of man has an extraordinary capacity for entering into its n-dimensional memory from a vast variety of starting points to search for data in it. I enjoy working with matrix (field) theory which in a small measure reflects a bit of this important human capacity.

Jokes may exploit negative expectancies of taxonomy or matrix shape or content, since man's mind can enjoy unexpected implications of shared characteristics. A cat, for example, cannot bark. If, however, one pretends that a specialist "bilingual" cat can do so, pleasure can be invoked, as in figure 13.5. Nonoccurrence of a feature leads to contrast (Chapter 6), which is crucial to the identification and understanding of the nature of units.

A theory based on just one taxonomy, just one partitioning of characteristics, treating the universe as entailing "nothing but" some one (clearly important) set of features, is in danger of *epistemological death*. *Formalism*, for example, is a useful way of describing certain differences between behavior patterns. But if meaning, relevance, purpose, and observer perspective are not directly provided for in the viewing model, mental blindness to the more complex nature of humanity may be the price paid for the temporary elegance of the taxonomy or mathematical rules.

# 14

# Universe of Discourse

A number of approaches, with overlapping components, relate to context. In Chapter 12, both form and meaning were simultaneously relevant. In Chapter 13 it was change which was in view, with no change occurring unless something contextual was shared. Now we speak of context in a much broader way, in relation to *universe of discourse*. This refers to the general or temporary or somewhat permanent *frame of reference*, either tacit or explicit, within which social interchange is taking place; it can include topic, style, genre, discipline, or general speaker or hearer expectancies. It can reflect the cohesion component of any tagmeme of the referential hierarchy, in relation to truth or falsehood, specific history, or specific or particular encyclopedic background; or it can include general relation to the situation in respect to space, time, society, or personal psychology; or it can include phonological cohesion factors of voice quality controlled by style or emotional situation; or it can include grammatical cohesion factors which control or are controlled by literary form. Such cohesion features of the hierarchies are touched upon in sections 11.4, 10.7, and 9.4–the latter with special reference to the tagmeme *as itself unit-in-context*.

In addition, distribution as an essential feature of an emic unit is treated extensively in Chapter 8. But the term "distribution" was there much more restricted than is universe of discourse. Distribution was referring to the paradigmatic occurrence of a set of units in a particular structure (or structures) occurring as in some place (or specific set of places) in such an explicit structure. Universe of discourse as a term refers rather to the broader background, often tacit, and often having relevance to a very wide variety of matters without explicit relation to their particular hierarchical structuring in particular units of grammar or phonology or reference, but having a pervasive influence on them all, without necessarily being tied to one particular level (or closed set of levels) or manifestations or constituents of those structures immediately at hand. So we are at a very high level of coherence of the human being in his joking or lying, his fears and his hates, his biography or his social immersion, his explicit assumptions or his unstated but controlling beliefs. Beyond the pure mathematician in his abstractions lies person in commitment to the sheer joy of the pattern chase. We too can have fun together, searching for evidence that the man in the street—not just the professional of some kind—is tacitly aware of, and exploits for pleasure, such "universes" accessible to him.

## 14.1 Lack of Coherence in Speaker-Hearer Interaction

When a speaker addresses his audience, he may expect it to expect something of what he himself expects. If the hearer does not do so, then communication may fail completely or go awry. By Ciardi (1959:847) this expectation is called the *sympathetic contract* in relation to poetry. For him, the relation between the one who writes the poem and the one who receives it must include a shared belief or value system, permanent or temporarily in the imagination, if the *artistic* event is to *occur*. Thus, he says, "the badness of bad poetry can always and only be located in the quality of the sympathetic contract." But the same expectancies affect prose writing and ordinary conversation.

If the speaker asks a question or makes a comment, awaiting a reply, he does so against the background of such expectations. If the hearer ignores this fact in replying, conversational chaos may engulf the original speaker. Figure 14.1 shows how the reply can answer the actual surface question but totally fail to meet the about-to-be-buried expectation.

In the implied universe of discourse here, Whippletree was speaking in a way which should have clued in Mr. Axelgrease that Whippletree *wanted a remedy* for his sick cow—not a mere answer to the surface question. Whippletree assumed that Axelgrease would assume that Whippletree wanted helpful medical advice—and acted accordingly, using the supposedly prescribed turps as a hoped-for remedy. When his cow died, he was puzzled—he had expected better advice from his friend. So he inquired again. The shock. Turps was not a remedy for Axelgrease, either. (Note, further, that in my reporting this old joke, I made up names to help signal the fact that I was back in a farming community: the whippletree, as a swinging bar tying traces to a cart, was normal to the universe of discourse of that community of sixty years ago before machines took over.)

In figure 14.2, on the other hand, the universe of discourse behind each question is noncoherent with that of the answer.

In figure 14.3 the speakers imply that there *is* a relation between two universes of discourse, by asking the hearer to *guess* some kind of unexpected relationship—and thus cuing a probable joke.

*Four weeks (and sixty years) ago: Mr. Whippletree asks Mr. Axelgrease:* Alex, what did you give yr'old cow when she was sick?
*Mr. Axelgrease:* Turps.
*Two weeks later:* Alex, what d'you say you gave yr'old cow when she was sick?
*Mr. Axelgrease:* Turps.
*Two weeks later still:* Alex, what d'you say you gave yr'old cow when she was sick?
*Mr. Axelgrease:* Turps.
*Mr. Whippletree:* Well I gave turps to mine, and she died!
*Mr. Axelgrease:* So'd mine.

*Figure 14.1. Failure of reply to meet expectations of speaker can give difficulty.*

A. *Medical professor:* What happens when a body is immersed in water?
   *Student:* The phone rings.
B. *Patient:* Doctor, what should I do if I get run down?
   *Doctor, harassed:* Take down the license number.
C. *Teacher:* Name me four members of the cat family.
   *Student:* Father cat, mother cat, brother cat, sister cat.

*Figure 14.2. Slippage of elicited universe of discourse can be deliberate, even in serious situations, for wry humor; or it may be through failure to understand. In A, a medical student is presumably trying to enjoy a joke at the professor's expense. In B, the doctor seems to have been pressed beyond endurance, and may have to start over for serious consultation. In C, a very young student may have been serious, but has failed to learn the implicit taxonomic guidelines of the underlying class.*

A. *Query:* If you pour hot water down a rabbit hole, what do you get?
   *Answer:* Hot cross bunnies.

B. *Query:* Why is a moth flying around a lighted candle like a gate
   blowing in the wind?
   *Answer:* If it kéeps-ón-ít-sínges-its wíngs.
   *Or:* If it kéeps-ón-íts-hínges-it-swíngs.

*Figure 14.3. The speaker may imply a mixture of universes of discourse,
as in much humor. In A, the clause* What do you get, *in appropriate
contexts, invites the hearer to guess at some kind of association. A* hot
cross bun *is a biscuit marked with frosting in the shape of a cross, and
eaten by some groups at Easter time; the word* bun *ties the association
to the first syllable of* bunny, *as a pet name for* rabbit, *while* hot *reflects
the temperature of the water, and* cross *the annoyance of the wetted rabbit. In B, the answers can be homophonous, if pronounced rapidly and
smoothly, as suggested by the hyphens and stress marks.*

A. *One duck hunter to another, in the pouring rain:* Can you imagine my
   wife wanting me to go shopping in wet weather like this!

B. *One farmer to another:* I entered my mule in the Kentucky Derby. I
   didn't expect him to win, but I thought that the association might do
   him some good.

*Figure 14.4. Inconsistency with reality, as seen in us by others, can be
annoying or ludicrous. In A, a man sees rainy weather as a deterrent to
shopping but not to hunting; the wife is expected to disapprove the dis-
tinction. In B, the farmer suggests that a mule may receive a good influence, by associating with the right company; we are expected to doubt it.*

## 14.2. Failure of Coherence of Speaker with Reality as Seen by Others

As we listen to a person's statements, they may appear to us
to be inconsistent. In figure 14.4, the first illustration portrays a man as
inconsistent, in that he reacts differently to comparable circumstances; in
the second, a man humorously suggests the improbable relevance of an
association.

In figure 14.5, fiction exploits expectancies of a politico-social universe of

*Figure 14.5. Political coherence can be lost, with disastrous social consequences. Here the fictional character Rip Van Winkle does not know that times have changed, since he has just wakened from years of blissful, loyal sleep.*

discourse, by showing how Rip Van Winkle got into trouble when he tried to be politically polite and loyal, but was interpreted—having been asleep for many years and not knowing that there had been a change of political climate in the meantime—as being hostile to unrecognized-as-new government.

## 14.3. Behavioral Universals in Language Learning

In one sense, all languages are equivalent: any one of them is thoroughly adequate for its native speakers to discuss anything which interested their grandfathers. And any of these can be expanded to include adequate reference to any new topic or item, provided it is given time enough and provided that not too many new items are thrust at it from the outside at any one period. (When an industrialized culture, however, *first* contacts a nonindustrialized one, the many new concepts and accompanying correlative vocabulary items may give it a verbal traffic jam. The capacity to develop or to borrow new terms is a *universal* of human experience, in all languages.

Another factor which is universal is that all cultures must *talk about* many items which are related to their survival. In all cultures people must eat to live. All cultures must recruit new members. All must have role differentiation, communication, shared cognitive orientations and goals, and regulation of disruptive behavior, as well as means of socialization—that is, the induction of an individual into the roles and subsystems of the society (see Aberle et al. 1950). It is reliance on these factors which makes it practical for a person to assume, when he visits a culture which has a language which has never been written (of which there are many in fact still in existence), to assume that it will be a normal or ordinary language (not the language of birds or beasts), and to assume that he can find shared bridges of behavior over which he can pass to learn it. And it is these facts which have allowed me for many years to be willing to try in an hour, in public, to start learning a language by gesture only (that is, in a *monolingual demonstration*, without using English or any other language shared by the other party to the demonstration). Many colleagues of the Summer Institute of Linguistics have also given such demonstrations repeatedly. (For one on TV videotape, see Pike 1977, Program 5.)

## 14.4. Why Translation Is Possible

It is only the presence of such behavioral universals which makes it other than a wild dream to assume that translation from any one language to any other should be *expected* as being possible. *Translation* may for our purposes here be considered a special instance of *cross-cultural paraphrase*. From this viewpoint many things which have been mentioned earlier in this volume become helpful in understanding why translation is possible at all between cultures which seem so different on the surface.

Every culture has its own "theories"—its cultural windows as ways of looking at the world as a particular set of universes of discourse; and just as in our culture people can talk together (somewhat) even if they differ as to assumptions, so they can learn to talk across language differences. In each there can be misunderstandings; in each, different presuppositions can block, temporarily or permanently, appreciation for a viewpoint (Chapter 1). In each, there will be differences of observer perspective (static, dynamic, and relational as basic ones, chapters 3–5). In each there will be systems of contrast (Chapter 6) and areas of variation (Chapter 7), so that emic units must be identified for each before clear understanding can be achieved. For each there will be a particular set of units of grammatical and phonological types (chapters 9–10) which must be mastered, for transfer of concepts into the relevant form, in order to have viable and expressible form-meaning composites (Chapter 12).

But the nonlinguist may still wonder how it is possible to use words in a translation when the words in the second language never mean *exactly* what they mean in the first. It is important to see that here, also, this translation problem is not different in principle from that facing the English speaker who enters a new discipline—say that of linguistics. One can get formal, logical definitions of new technical terms in relation to including genus and differentiating species (see fig. 13.4); or one can learn the terms through a set of illustrations, or from a book-length discussion.

In general, however, the way we normally learn the meaning of new words is by hearing them in contexts. For the moment, it may be helpful to think of a new word as a partial vacuum into which flows meaning from the environment. As it is heard in more and more environments, the word picks up more and more marginal meanings. Notice that a large dictionary gives not only definitions of words but samples excerpted from various writings. In fact it is the study of the contexts of the excerpts which leads the lexicographer to make the definition, not the definition which leads to the meanings.

This implies that a *context has very high power to determine or to change a meaning*—vastly greater than would be suspected until we have studied the matter (see fig. 14.6). That contexts can form or change meanings is a very legitimate and valuable (in fact crucial) characteristic of language.

It allows for the adaptations of ordinary vocabulary for scientific purposes or for the discussion of new culture habits. Translation, furthermore,

I have some good property: *hold in possession*
It has three parts: *consists of*
I have a letter to write: *obligation*
I have enemies: *stand in relationship to*
I had bad news: *received*
He had the gall to refuse: *characterized by*
I had a cold: *experienced*
I had a fight: *performed*
I had an opinion: *entertained in mind*
I had the children stay: *caused to*
We'll have no more of that: *allow*
He had only a little French: *was competent in*
We had him, then: *in position of disadvantage*
He had been had by his partner: *put at disadvantage*
I had my rights: *able to exercise them*
She had a baby: *bore*
They had dinner: *partook of*
They can be had for a price: *bribed*

*Figure 14.6. Dictionaries use context to reach definitions of words. From such citation forms, the lexicographer can deduce the usage of forms and their elicited impact on behavior or understanding (data adapted from Webster's 1963). This is possible only because contexts in part shape meanings.*

is a special instance of the modification of terms by context; terms never quite match across the two languages, but the new contexts of the translated document may bring sufficient change to the starting meanings of the words used to allow them to communicate with a degree of accuracy sufficient for the purposes of the facts or behavior discussed. On the other hand, the word *sincere* normally means 'free from dissimulation, not pretending that which is false'; but if one says *Always be sincere*, followed immediately by the addition of *whether you mean it or not* (as on a joking postcard), the added context forces *sincere* to mean the opposite (that is, as presenting a false front of apparent integrity even when there is none). It is almost impossible to resist the implication of that change in such a context. Such contextual power can appear to an observer as damaging or constructive, or as diabolical or heavenly, depending on his estimate of the legitimacy and local usefulness of the change elicited.

Items being translated, furthermore, presumably have contexts unfamiliar to the new readers, or else there would have been no reason to translate them. And the contexts new to the readers must themselves elicit sufficient change in the meanings of the words used to allow for the transfer of meaning across the initial culture gap.

## 14.5. Poetry Can Concentrate the Signaling of a Universe of Discourse

Concentration of features of contrasting universes of discourse are found in humor, as we have seen in illustrations already given in this chapter. Poetry can do the same, but even more subtly. In figure 14.7 a tiny poem of E. E. Cummings combines the use of orthography, line spacing, and brief lexical content to suggest a whole social-political setting. My phonetic interpretation of the data has been heavily influenced by the work of Axelrod (1944:89).

Graphically, in the last line there, by spelling *pause* as "paws", the author suggests a relation to the first line, where *applause* is spelled as "applaws." Since applause is made by hands, and since "paws" are the hands of animals, the heavy nature of the applause is forced on the reader. The separate lines suggest separate stress groups—two stresses for *fellow*, in lines two and three, and two stresses for *citizens* in lines four and five. The "isn'ts" suggests an unvoiced ending of *citizens*—which in turn suggests a foreigner speaking English. This, further, implies that the stress groups are foreign also, lacking sufficient *non*stress on the last syllables of *fellow* and *citizens*. Granted these interpretations, the *occasion* emerges: there is a patriotic celebration with an appropriate address. The speaker addresses the audience as one with them. But he is a naturalized citizen, still retaining a

> applaws)
>
> fell
> ow
> sit
> isn'ts"
>
> (a paw s
>      e.e. cummings

*Figure 14.7. Poetry may concentrate signals identifying a universe of discourse. (Copyright 1944 by E. E. Cummings; renewed 1972 by Nancy T. Andrews. Reprinted from* Complete Poems 1913–1962 *by permission of Harcourt Brace Jovanovich, Inc.).*

foreign accent; and sometimes a new member of the national family can feel more deeply patriotic on such occasions than a person born into it. Thus an extraordinary hint is given in brief compass of an extensive background, an interlocking set of elements signaling a universe of discourse.

## 14.6. Conclusion: Unit-in-Context within Context

No unit relevant to human beings exists without its having a relation to a system of interlocking types of context. The units exist in a vast matrix of n-dimensional intersecting relations within which the specific unit is distributed and which comprise our universe with our cognitive frames of reference.

This contextual factor gives the tagmeme its alternate technical name— *unit-in-context*. Each tagmeme (see sections 9.4–5) involves four kinds of contextual distribution of a unit, any one of which can be under temporary focus. At any one moment it is manifested by one element of a set of elements (in Cell 2, Class) such that any one member of the set is substitutable for that member of that set in that context without changing any *structural* characteristic of the *kind* of pattern of which it is a part. Yet that set of elements is a part of an immediately larger pattern, which contains it and which it helps make up; and the part comes in a particular functional place (Cell 1, Slot) in relation to that larger pattern. But that function has a relevance, significance, purpose (Cell 3, Role) relative to the action or observation or judgment of an observer of that unit. And the unit is embedded in a larger set of general kinds of backgrounds (Cell 4, Cohesion), a referential set of beliefs, situations, precedents, biographies, histories, logic, sanity or lunacy, science or fiction, seriousness or humor, observation or imagination, and others; and these help hold units together in a coherent observer viewpoint, or in a set of happenings or things or causal relations and controls. Similarly, there may be both grammatical patterns of agreement or contrast, and phonological ones.

A unit-in-context may be observed at any level of any one of the hierarchies. They comprise part of the warp and woof of every grammatical, generalized linear pattern of verbal or nonverbal patterns of behavior.

No hierarchy exists except in relation to the others. No *simple* necessary single mapping relation is present between the hierarchies of tagmemes. No simple set of rules is adequate to capture all the possibilities or to predict at one particular moment which choice will be made by the observers involved. If one wishes his theory to handle this human flexibility, he must allow his theory to have some *indeterminacy of choice* at the moment under observation. The theory must be able to *describe* any one variation of interaction, after it has occurred, without being forced to *predict* in advance which one must inevitably occur.

This points up a crucial assumption of the theory: Personal interaction is given priority over identification of things or abstractions. It is *persons* who perceive, imagine, and sense relations. It is persons who talk about these concepts. But persons have limits. Therefore they *must* have hierarchy, and hierarchy intersecting with hierarchy. *Only thus* can they signal the needed complexity of their experience, and do so in a way that will not stifle them.

# References

Note: For extensive documentation and discussion of tagmemic theory in historical perspective, see Pike 1967a; for bibliography on grammatical methodological matters in tagmemics, see Pike and Pike 1977. For this current volume, where the general background principles (rather than their sources) are being presented, it seems inappropriate to duplicate the prior discussion. The references given here, therefore, are largely those from which illustrations are taken—and these, in turn, are usually drawn from data with which I have had direct or indirect contact. A few—but only a few—further references are to materials which I refer to or quote from directly, as supplementary to my own experience or to the earlier documentation just referred to.

Aberle, D. F., A. K. Cohen, A. K. Davis, M. J. Levy, Jr., and F. X. Sutton. 1950. The functional prerequisites of a society. Ethics 60.100–111.

Aschmann, Herman P. 1946. Totonaco phonemes. International journal of American linguistics 12.34–43.

Axelrod, Joseph. 1944. Cummings and phonetics. Poetry 65.11.88–94.

Bloomfield, Leonard. 1933. Language. New York: Holt, Rinehart and Winston.

Brend, Ruth M. 1968. A tagmemic analysis of Mexican Spanish clauses. The Hague: Mouton.

Browning, Robert. 1895. The complete poetic and dramatic works of Robert Browning. Cambridge, Mass.: Houghton Mifflin.

Carnap, Rudolf. [1939] 1955. Foundations of logic and mathematics. Foundations of the unity of science: toward an international encyclopedia of unified science, ed. Otto Neurath, Rudolf Carnap, and Charles Morris, 1:139–214. Chicago: University of Chicago Press.

Chomsky, Noam. 1957. Syntactic structures. The Hague: Mouton.

———. 1962. A transformational approach to syntax. Third Texas conference on problems of linguistic analysis in English, May 9–12, 1958, 124–69. Austin: University of Texas.

———. 1966. Cartesian linguistics: a chapter in the history of rationalist thought. New York: Harper and Row.

Ciardi, John. 1959. How does a poem mean? An introduction to literature, pt. 3. Boston: Houghton Mifflin Co.

Fillmore, Charles J. 1968. The case for case. Universals in linguistic theory, ed. by Emmon Bach and Robert Harms, 1–80. New York: Holt, Rinehart and Winston.

Fischer-Jørgensen, Eli. 1975. Trends in phonological theory: a historical introduction. Copenhagen: Akademisk Forlag.

Frank, Philip. 1957. Philosophy of science: the link between science and philosophy. Englewood Cliffs, N.J.: Prentice-Hall.

Fries, Charles C. 1952. The structure of english. New York: Harcourt Brace.

Gelb, I. J. [1952] 1963. A study of writing. 2d ed. Chicago: University of Chicago Press.

Howland, Lilian G. 1981. Communicational integration of reality and fiction. Language and communication 1.89–148.

Hyman, Larry. 1975. Phonology: theory and analysis. New York: Holt, Rinehart and Winston.

Jespersen, Otto. 1937. Analytic syntax. Copenhagen: Munksgaard.

Jones, Linda K. 1977. Theme in english expository discourse. Edward Sapir monograph series in language, culture, and cognition 2. Lake Bluff, Ill.: Jupiter Press.

Joyce, James. [1916] 1968. A portrait of the artist as a young man. New York: Viking Press.

Kaplan, J. D., ed. 1952. Dialogues of Plato. Trans. by Benjamin Jowett. New York: Pocket Books.

Kuhn, Thomas S. 1962. The structure of scientific revolutions. Chicago: University of Chicago Press.

Lamb, Sydney. 1964. The sememic approach to structural semantics. Transcultural studies in cognition, ed. by A. Kimball Romney and Roy G. D'Andrade, 57–58. American anthropologist, vol. 66, no. 3, part 2, special publication.

Langer, Susanne K. [1937] 1953. An introduction to symbolic logic. 2d ed. New York: Dover.

Miller, George A. 1956. The magical number seven, plus or minus two: some limits on our capacity for processing information. Psychological review 63.81–97.

Moser, Edward, and Mary B. Moser. 1965. Consonant vowel balance in Seri (Hokan) syllables. Linguistics 16.50–67.

Nida, Eugene A. 1975. Componential analysis of meaning: an introduction to semantic structures. The Hague: Mouton.

Patrick, G. T. W., Trans. [1888] 1889. The fragments of the work of Heraclitus of Ephesus on nature: translation from the Greek text of Bywater. Baltimore: Murray.

Pickett, Velma. 1960. Hierarchical structure of Isthmus Zapotec. Language dissertation no. 56. Baltimore: Linguistic Society of America.

Pike, Eunice V. 1970. Review Aspects of phonological theory, by Paul M. Postal. Lingua 25.30–46.

Pike, Kenneth L. 1945. The intonation of American English. University of Michigan publications in linguistics no. 1. Ann Arbor: University of Michigan Press.

———. 1948. Tone languages: A technique for determining the number and type of pitch contrasts in a language, with studies in tonemic substitution and fusion. University of Michigan publications in linguistics no. 4. Ann Arbor: University of Michigan Press.

———. 1952. Operational phonemics in reference to linguistic relativity. Journal of the acoustic society of America 24.618–25.

———. 1957. Abdominal pulse types in some Peruvian languages. Language 33.30–35.

———. 1962. Dimensions of grammatical constructions. Language 38.221–44.

———. 1963. Theoretical implications of matrix permutation in Fore (New Guinea). Anthropological linguistics 5.8.1–23.

———. 1964a. Name fusions as high-level particles in matrix theory. Linguistics 6.83–91.

———. 1964b. On the grammar of intonation. Proceedings of the fifth international congress of phonetic sciences, 105–19.

———. 1965. Language—where science and poetry meet. College English 26.283–92.

———. [1954, 1955, 1960] 1967a. Language in relation to a unified theory of the structure of human behavior. 2d ed. The Hague: Mouton.

———. 1967b. Tongue-root position in practical phonetics. Phonetica 17.129–40.

———. 1967c. Stir, change, create: poems and essays. Grand Rapids, Mich.: Eerdmans.

———. 1977. Pike on language. (Series: 3/4-inch videocassettes [NTSC standard] and 16mm kinescopes.) Ann Arbor: University of Michigan Television Center. Program no. 1: Voices at work [phonetics]; Program no. 2: The music of speech [pitch and poetry]; Program no. 3: Waves of change [the how and why of change in language]; Program no. 4: The way we know—the value of theory in linguistics study; Program no. 5: Into the unknown [learning an unknown language by gesture—a monolingual demonstration].

———. 1981. Tagmemics, discourse, and verbal art. Michigan studies in the humanities.

Pike, Kenneth L., and Evelyn G. Pike. 1977. Grammatical analysis. Summer Institute of Linguistics publications in linguistics 53. [2d ed., with section references—but not page numbers—unchanged, 1982.]

Potter, Ralph K., George A. Kopp, and Harriet C. Green. 1947. Visible speech. New York: Van Nostrand.

Robbins, Frank E. 1961. Quiotepec syllable patterning. International journal of American linguistics 27.237–50.

Stahlke, Herbert, and Ruth M. Brend. 1967. The use of matrices in the preparation of language textbooks. Language learning 17.37–44.

Stewart, J. M. 1967. Tongue-position in Akan vowel harmony. Phonetica 16.185–204.

Suharno, Ignatious, and Kenneth L. Pike. 1976. From Baudi to Indonesian. Irian Jaya: Cenderawashi University and Summer Institute of Linguistics.

Tench, Paul. 1976. Double ranks in a phonological hierarchy. Journal of linguistics 12.1–20.

Webster's seventh new collegiate dictionary. 1963. Springfield, Mass. G. & L. Merriam Co.

Wilder, Thornton N. [1931] 1963. The long Christmas dinner. New York: Harper & Row.

# Index